NIALL C. HARRINGTON was born in Dublin, on 23 January 1901, the day on which his father was elected to the Lord Mayoralty of Dublin, the first of three terms. His parents were T. C. Harrington, MP, BL, a native of Castletownbere in County Cork, and Elizabeth O'Neill, the daughter of Doctor and Mrs Edward O'Neill of Dublin.

After the death of his parents, he went to live with his uncle in Tralee, where he attended the Christian Brothers school, later going on to Rockwell College in Cashel. He decided to take up pharmacy as a career and was apprenticed to a chemist in Boyle, County Roscommon, but was forced to leave the area in 1920 because of his involvement in IRA activities. He joined the new Free State Army shortly after its inception in 1921, initially in the medical corps, but after the outbreak of the Civil War he transferred for infantry service in the Dublin Guards.

He was promoted from corporal to 2nd lieutenant after the Droum ambush in Kerry in August 1922, and was appointed Captain and Adjutant, 27th Infantry Battalion, on its formation in Kenmare in 1923. In the course of service he became Adjutant 54th Battalion, Newbridge, County Kildare, and 25th Battalion, Curragh and Athlone; Staff Officer 2nd Bureau GHQ; Training Officer OCT, and later Staff Officer Military Section; Commandant Marine and Coast Watching Service; OC Marine Service, Haulbowline, County Cork; Command Intelligence Officer, Eastern Command; Command Adjutant Eastern Command, and finally Staff Officer and Deputy to Director G2 Branch GHQ.

On his retirement in 1959, he was appointed National Organizer of the Federated Union of Employers, a position he held from 1959 to 1974. He was President and Secretary of the Parnell Commemoration Society, and wrote numerous newspaper articles and radio scripts. He was a frequent broadcaster on behalf of the Army.

He died in 1981.

NIALL C. HARRINGTON

KERRY
LANDING

ANVIL BOOKS LIMITED

Published 1992 by
Anvil Books Limited
45 Palmerston Road, Dublin 6

ISBN 0 947962 70 0

Typesetting by Computertype
Printed in Ireland by Colour Books

TO MY FRIEND OF MANY YEARS,
DAN NOLAN
WITHOUT WHOSE HELP, ADVICE AND
ENCOURAGEMENT THIS MEMOIR
WOULD NEVER HAVE SEEN THE
LIGHT OF DAY

There seems to be a malignant fate dogging the fortunes of Ireland; for at every critical period in her story the man whom the country trusts and follows is taken from her. It was so with Thomas Davis and Parnell, and now with Arthur Griffith.

MICHAEL COLLINS
August 1922

Poor Ireland! all this is a pity. It never should have happened.

LIAM LYNCH
as he lay mortally wounded, 10 April 1923

CONTENTS

ILLUSTRATIONS

between pages 64 and 65

between pages 128 and 129

Photographs 6, 7, 15, 16 and 17 are from the Lawrence Collection in the National Library of Dublin.
Maps by permission of the Ordnance Survey, permit 5539.

ACKNOWLEDGEMENTS

On behalf of my father, Niall Harrington, I would like to make some acknowledgements.

I am deeply indebted to the people in Kerry who helped him in every way, especially Dan Nolan, his great friend and colleague, who worked so hard on the editing of this book, and Con Casey who supplied invaluable information and who is, I know, looking forward to its publication.

I would also like to thank Commandant Peter Young of Military Archives, who has been a tower of strength; Dr Pat Donlon of the National Library and her staff, particularly Noel Kissane; Kathleen Browne and everyone at Kerry County Library; the Archives Department of University College, Dublin; and Rena Dardis of Anvil Books for her commitment and dedication to the publishing of *Kerry Landing*.

I must add some words of gratitude to my friends who helped me greatly: Dan King, Louis McRedmond, Pat Butler, Brian and Martha MacManus, Hazel Smyth, Paddy Dunne, and — for their patient typing and retyping — Nessie Bergin, Mary Archer, Rosemary O'Boyle and Joan Logan. Last, but not least, my thanks to my husband Brendan for, as always, his unfailing support.

My father intended *Kerry Landing* to be a memorial to all who died on both sides of this tragic war. I hope that everyone who reads it will recognize it as such.

Nuala Jordan

INTRODUCTION

This introduction is intended as an explanatory background to the events leading up to the IRA split of 1922, and was written by the author shortly before his death in 1981.

The Easter Rising of 1916 was a failure. But the execution of the leaders and the internment of the rank and file kindled a spark that could not be put out. The Volunteers had risen from the ashes of Easter week and under threat of the Conscription Act of April 1918 (which would have forced Irishmen to enlist in the British Army) reorganized and regrouped themselves; the Act was not enforced.

In December 1918, Sinn Féin won a decisive victory in the General Election, winning 73 of the 105 seats. It was a vote for national independence. And during the following year the Minister for Defence in the new government, Cathal Brugha, brought together the various Volunteer groups to create an army which swore allegiance to the republic. Thus was born the Irish Republican Army, the IRA.

On 21 January 1919 the first Dáil Éireann assembled in the Mansion House, Dublin. Eamon de Valera (then in Lincoln jail, from which he was to escape the following March) was elected President.

That same day the first shots of what became known as the War of Independence were fired at Soloheadbeg in County Tipperary, when Dan Breen and members of his battalion ambushed a consignment of explosives; two policemen were killed. It was to continue until July 1921.

THE TRUCE

Early in June 1921 there was a rumour afloat that negotiations were taking place for a cease fire. The idea was welcomed by both sides and the Truce finally took effect from 11 July 1921. When conflict ceased at noon on that July day, the Irish were war-weary and apprehensive about the future. In Dublin, General Headquarters of the IRA had been experiencing ever-increasing difficulty in hiding administrative offices and in communicating with countrywide units. Increased British military presence in the city had intensified the problems of the Dublin Brigade active service units. Whole streets were being sealed off with barbed wire entanglements preparatory to a comb-out of every house by troops. Some dumps had been discovered and large quantities of munitions seized. Thousands of IRA men from all parts of the country, many of the best officers included, were in jails or internment camps, some awaiting execution. There was an acute shortage of arms and ammunition in every brigade. Plans to import a shipload of arms from Italy had foundered, but forty-nine Thompson submachine-guns with 500 rounds per gun were smuggled in from the United States early in the Truce.[1]

The active service situation in the provinces at the cessation of hostilities can be more easily understood by the disclosure of Commandant-General Tom Barry, most famous of all column commanders, that 'at the Truce our armament (3rd West Cork Brigade) was some 110 rifles, one Lewis machine-gun, one Hotchkiss light machine-gun sent by Collins after Crossbarry, hand-guns, and a continuous shortage of ammunition.'[2] In addition, 'we had not more than 300 properly trained and experienced fighting men.'[3] For a further assessment of the situation one can turn to the findings of David Fitzpatrick's political research in Clare. 'Even after the Truce,' he wrote, 'at the end of September 1921, there were only 158 rifles in the county in IRA hands — 73 in the east, 71 in mid-Clare and 14 in the west. Of these, 12 were miniatures, others not in service order, and all seriously short of ammunition. An additional 372 shot-guns and 178 revolvers completed the armament of Clare IRA.'[4]

In June 1921 (the month before the Truce), when the muster roll of Liam Lynch's 1st Southern Division was 30,620 officers and men, its entire armament consisted of 578 modern rifles, eleven light machine-guns, over a thousand revolvers and pistols and a large number of shot-guns. Rifle and machine-gun ammunition was 'dangerously low'.[5] The division then comprised eleven brigades: five in Cork, three in Kerry, two in Waterford and one in west Limerick.

As to Tom Barry's statement that there were not more than 300 properly trained and experienced fighting men in the West Cork Brigade at the Truce, one has to appreciate that he was a perfectionist in his assessment of combat capabilities. Besides, his column had, as had all active IRA units, a back-up of hundreds of Volunteers whose essential tasks included guard duties, intelligence, road blocking, scouting, signalling, maintenance of supplies and communications. Cumann na mBan, the women's organization, carried dispatches, scouted, provided first aid, nursing and safe houses for the sick and wounded.

The British also had their problems. There was a serious weakening of morale amongst the troops, whose social life was totally disrupted by restriction of movement from barrack quarters and whose day to day expectation could not exclude being at the receiving end of a bullet or a bomb. The necessity for constant vigilance was having its effect. Resultant breaches of discipline found outlet in the torture of prisoners and the wrecking of property, both public and private. In a memorandum to the Cabinet dated 24 May 1921, the Commander-in-Chief in Ireland, General Sir Nevil Macready, underlined the stress and strain which the nature of the Irish war imposed on both officers and men. 'Unless I am entirely mistaken,' he wrote, 'the present state of affairs in Ireland, so far as regards the troops serving there, must be brought to a conclusion by October, or steps must be taken to relieve practically the whole of the troops together with the great majority of the commanders and their staff.'[6]

At Cabinet level there was a crucial question of policy as to whose responsibility it was — that of the military or the police — to hold on to Ireland as an integral part of the British Empire. The Prime Minister, David Lloyd George, insisted at the Cabinet of 2 June 1921 that 'the Irish job ... was a policeman's job supported by the military and not vice versa. So long as it becomes a military job only it will fail.'[7]

The Royal Irish Constabulary was no longer functioning as a civic police force. The members were well-armed paramilitaries but were not subject to military law. Some 4,000 resignations, retirements, dismissals and casualties had resulted in the recruitment in England of 9,000 British ex-service men for the force — the hated Black and Tans, whose only training was for war. The first of the Tans arrived in the spring of 1920. They were followed over from England in the autumn of that year by the even more notorious Auxiliaries, ex-British Army officers whose sole purpose was to terrorize the Irish into submission. At the Truce, the strength of the RIC exceeded 15,000 officers and men, of whom little more than one-third were Irish. Lloyd George and Winston Churchill had been satisfied to let them have their heads to murder, burn, rob and loot at will. One result of such licence, and their heavy drinking, was that the entire police force was completely demoralized and beyond control by July 1921.

Under mounting pressure to determine the issue of whether 'the Irish job' was one for the police or the military, the Cabinet, on 2 June, agreed to wage a military campaign on an extensive scale against the IRA, commencing on 14 July. The decision meant that martial law would be declared over the entire twenty-six counties of 'Southern Ireland', and the administration of the area handed over to the British Army to be treated as 'a zone of battle'.[8] Accordingly, the Irish command was immediately reinforced by seventeen infantry battalions, and two mounted rifle regiments. Additional reinforcements consisting of cavalry, marine and tank corps forces were planned for mid-July.[9] The projected military strength in the martial law area was 'a hundred thousand new special troops and police and thousands of armoured cars.'[10] The military plans provided for identity controls and an aggressive land blockade, involving the building of cordons of blockhouses linked with barbed wire, in a system of widespread search and destroy. Churchill, who, as Secretary of State for War, would be the minister responsible for this 'new drive policy', believed that it could be implemented and that Parliament would be ready to uphold the Government in giving effect to it. Field Marshal Sir Henry Wilson, who, as Chief of the Imperial General Staff, had expressed his thoughts on the necessity for a 'clean-cut policy on shooting by roster',[11] was urging the confiscation of all motor-cars, bicycles and horses, and the closure of every bank and post-office, together with the suppression of 'hostile newspapers'. Closure of the ports by naval blockage was under Cabinet consideration. (The British plans came to public knowledge during the Truce.)

The Truce gave the Irish people relief from ever-present fear as well as the prospect of a return to normal living. It also gave the IRA the opportunity to arm, train and recruit for a resumption of the war on a more intensive scale, circumstances in which it could be regarded as an instrument of mixed blessings. In its wake there came an influx of thousands of men into the IRA, and in the overall their numbers were not to its advantage, as they were too difficult to control.

THE TREATY

On 6 December 1921, 'Articles for Agreement of a [Peace] Treaty' were signed in London by a team of five Irish plenipotentiaries led by Arthur Griffith, and the plenipotentiaries of the British Government led by the Prime Minister, David Lloyd George.

The effect of the Treaty was to set up a self-governing Irish state in the twenty-six counties that the British called 'Southern Ireland', with a Government elected by the people of the new state and responsible only to them. The Treaty was received in Ireland with mixed feelings. There were objectionable clauses. In particular, everybody hated partition. Nevertheless, the overwhelming opinion was that, except for the black blot of partition, it was a far better settlement than had been expected. The great majority of the people saw it as a tremendous achievement. They wanted the Treaty accepted and worked. (Of historical interest is this quote from Tom Barry, written many years after the events under discussion: 'It is a fact that when the June 1922 elections came and the issue was the Treaty [sic], which did not give them the Republic, or renewed war with the British, West Cork voted overwhelmingly for the pro-Treaty candidates. The same results obtained throughout the country in all areas where the IRA had been active against the British.'[12] — this from a man who opposed the Treaty and proposed instead a resumption of the Anglo-Irish war.)

Article 17 of the Treaty required that steps should be 'taken forthwith' for constituting a Provisional Government to which the British would hand over the authority, powers and machinery of government pending the establishment of the Free State by legislation passed in Dáil Éireann and the British Parliament.

The Treaty was immediately denounced by President de Valera and he led a Cabinet minority of one (three to four) against it; contrary to all expectations, he had decided to remain in Dublin rather than lead the plenipotentiaries.

Though the Treaty was ratified on 16 December by very big majorities in both Houses of Parliament at Westminster, its passage through Dáil Éireann was marked by the most acrimonious debates, which extended over fourteen days until 7 January 1922, when the Dáil, by the narrow majority of seven, 64 votes to 57, approved the articles. On 9 January, de Valera resigned as President. He immediately offered himself for re-election, but was defeated by two votes by Griffith, who became President of Dáil Éireann and at once nominated a pro-Treaty Cabinet.

Accordingly, the pro-Treaty deputies and the four representatives of Dublin University, meeting at the Mansion House, Dublin, on 14 January 1922, but refusing to acknowledge that they were the House of Commons of Southern Ireland provided by an Act of the British Parliament, formally ratified the Treaty and elected a Provisional Government. They met in the absence of de Valera and the other anti-Treaty members of Dáil Éireann, all of whom had refused to attend.[13] The IRA leaders opposed to the Treaty claimed that the pro-Treaty deputies had no right to use their membership of the Dáil for such purpose.

Two Irish governments now functioned side by side in the twenty-six counties: the Dáil Éireann Government, which remained in existence with Arthur Griffith as President, and the Provisional Government, of which Michael Collins was Chairman. Griffith was not a member of the Provisional

Government at this stage, but four members of the Dáil Cabinet were also Ministers in the Provisional Government. Unless the Treaty was rejected at the polls in the meantime, the Provisional Government would hold office and govern until 6 December 1922, when it would cease to exist with the formal establishment of Saorstat Éireann, the Irish Free State; its powers, laws and regulations would then automatically transfer to the Free State Government.

In that confused and emotive period in our history, not only were there two national governments functioning side by side; there were also two national armies where previously there had been only one, each giving allegiance to a republic: one to 'the existing republic' proclaimed on Easter Monday 1916 and ratified by Dáil Éireann on 21 January 1919, the other to a republic to be achieved in time by the 'stepping-stone' of the Treaty.

On 1 February 1922, the first uniformed contingent of the new army, numbering forty-six officers and men under the command of Captain Paddy O'Daly, marched through Dublin to Beggars' Bush barracks. As they marched past the City Hall the salute was taken by Arthur Griffith and Michael Collins. In Beggars' Bush barracks, which they took over from the Auxiliary Division of the Royal Irish Constabulary, they were addressed by General Richard Mulcahy, Minister for Defence, and the Chief of Staff, General Eoin O'Duffy. The Tricolour of the Saorstat was hoisted over the barracks by one of O'Daly's men. Thus was inaugurated the Irish Army of today.

The Tans and Auxiliaries had begun to clear out of their posts in the provinces immediately after the Dáil had approved the Treaty in January 1922. Disbandment of the old RIC took place gradually from late February but would not be complete until August. As a result, there was no police force in some areas, and in others not more than a token presence of the RIC or of the old republican police that had stemmed from the IRA.

The Civic Guard, an unarmed force (although the early trainees were drilled and instructed in the use of firearms), would not begin to operate effectively throughout the entire state until well into 1923. Inevitably, in the absence of effective policing or no policing at all, there was a sharp increase in crime carried out by armed criminal gangs, as often as not in the name of the IRA. It followed a familiar pattern of vengeful killings, settling of old scores, armed robbery, burning, looting and land grabbing. Whole communities were living in terror of the criminals. Over a hundred Protestant families fled west Cork after a series of sectarian killings in which ten male Protestants were shot dead. Faced with the urgent need to restore law and order and maintain it, a well-armed Criminal Investigation Department was organized by Collins and given a free hand to deal with criminals as part of its duties. The 'Oriel House men', as the CID came to be called, put down crime with ruthless efficiency.

Pseudo patriots and 'trucers' were also active. There were attacks on British servicemen preparing to vacate the country. Unarmed and retired RIC men were easy targets. Between December 1921 and the following February, more than eighty attacks on the RIC were recorded, leaving twelve dead. The murderous attacks continued into the summer.[14]

THE IRA SPLIT

The Irish Republican Army had split on the issue of the Treaty. Nine members of General Headquarters Staff were in favour and four against. Ten divisions were anti-Treaty and eight pro-Treaty. No division was totally pro-Treaty or anti-Treaty, and this was also true of the two Dublin brigades (Dublin and South Dublin), although the commandants of both had declared against the Treaty. Oscar Traynor, OC Dublin Brigade, had taken the anti-Treaty side, but he did not have the support of Tom Ennis, commandant of the 2nd Eastern Division, nor did he carry the vitally important Dublin Active Service Unit, which then included the Squad. The ASU under Paddy O'Daly remained almost completely loyal to Collins. In the south and west, Kerry was strongly influenced by Austin Stack, Cork by Liam Lynch, Sligo by Liam Pilkington, Limerick and part of Tipperary by Ernie O'Malley and Seamus

Robinson (but not the East Limerick Brigade and flying column, first of its kind in the War of Independence); they were in the main, anti-Treaty. The 4th Northern, OC Frank Aiken, was initially non-partisan, but took the anti-Treaty side soon after the Four Courts surrender on 30 June.

Sean MacEoin had the pro-Treaty adherence of Longford and Leitrim, as Michael Brennan had of Clare. Joe Sweeney led all four Donegal brigades to side with the Treaty.

In the spring of 1922, the anti-Treaty side of the IRA came into clear and open defiance of Dáil Éireann and the newly established Provisional Government.

On 11 January, a notice requesting an IRA convention on 26 March was served on General Mulcahy by senior anti-Treaty officers. It was signed by Rory O'Connor, Liam Mellows, Sean Russell and Seamus O'Donovan of the IRA (pre-Truce) General Headquarters Staff; divisional OCs Liam Lynch (1st Southern), Ernie O'Malley (2nd Southern), Joe McKelvey (3rd Northern), Tom Maguire (2nd Western), Liam Pilkington (3rd Western), Michael Kilroy (5th Western), brigade OCs Oscar Traynor (Dublin) and Andrew McDonnell (South Dublin). A stated objective of those who sought the convention was to repudiate the authority of the Dáil in relation to its control of the IRA and to place the IRA under the control of an Executive to be appointed by the convention.[15] Unequivocally this, in the prevailing circumstances, was a prescription for military dictatorship. An Acting Military Committee (later Council) IRA was set up by the signatories and other officers who shared their views, with Rory O'Connor as chairman; he was also the spokesman.

On 18 January, Richard Mulcahy arranged a meeting with the signatories to consider their request for the convention. Mulcahy presided and members of GHQ staff, the divisional commandants and commandants of brigades not yet linked in divisions were present. At the meeting Ernie O'Malley declared that he no longer recognized the authority of GHQ or Dáil Éireann. He would not obey any order from the Minister for Defence or his Chief of Staff.[16] His mutinous declaration had the immediate backing of Seamus O'Donovan and Liam Pilkington. In their eyes Michael Collins and Richard Mulcahy were traitors; they would have had both court-martialled for treason. O'Malley came to the meeting carrying two guns under his coat. 'I thought there would be an attempt to arrest some of our members,'[17] he explained, meaning some of the senior anti-Treaty officers.

The mood of the anti-Treaty IRA is best expressed in words written in 1917 by Liam Lynch, soon to become its Chief of Staff. 'We have declared for an Irish Republic,' he wrote, 'and will not live under any other law.'[18] Richard Mulcahy with equal fervour, was insisting that enlistment in the new army being formed by the Provisional Government was an engagement to serve in the 'Regular Forces of the Irish Republican Army'.[19] This was illusory, of course; *de facto* it was the army of the Provisional Government that was being recruited; in other words, it was the Free State Army. The IRA who were against the Treaty and recognized only 'the existing republic' could claim that theirs was the true Republican Army, and so they did claim.

On 18 February, Commandant Tomas Malone (alias Sean Forde), OC Mid-Limerick Brigade, published a proclamation repudiating the authority of GHQ and declaring the Chief of Staff a traitor.[20] A week later, units of O'Malley's 2nd Southern Division raided Clonmel police barracks, which the RIC were about to evacuate, and made a sensational seizure of arms and cars. The barracks had been used as a repository of RIC stores since mid-January and munitions and cars from many evacuated barracks were stored there pending shipment to England. The capture amounted to eleven motor-cars, 293 rifles and bayonets, 273 revolvers and pistols, three Lewis guns, forty-five shot-guns, 324,000 rounds of ammunition, 4,247 cartridges and sundry stores.[21] The munitions were removed in the police cars by O'Malley's men. They would reinforce his own line of opposition to the Treaty. About forty RIC men were made prisoners until the raid was over.

Seamus Robinson, OC 3rd Tipperary Brigade, suppressed the *Clonmel Nationalist*, which supported the Treaty. His men melted the type, smashed the machines and threatened the editor. He was not one for free speech that was not in line with his thinking. Rory O'Connor, for the same reason, had similar treatment in store for the *Freeman's Journal*. The pro-Treaty *Cork Examiner* was forced to publish a 'proclamation' denouncing the Treaty.

The most serious episode of that February, one that had direct bearing on the banning of the convention, was an army crisis in Limerick city. The city was in Malone's Mid-Limerick Brigade area which belonged to O'Malley's 2nd Southern Division. It was a most important strategic position on the Shannon and was about to be evacuated by the British.

Malone's proclamation alerted GHQ to the immediate danger of the vacated barracks being occupied by anti-Treaty elements of the IRA. Eoin O'Duffy took the only sensible course in dealing with the situation. He sent senior pro-Treaty officers — James Slattery, William Stapleton and Tom Kehoe, formerly of Michael Collins's Squad — to Limerick with orders to take over the Strand barracks and the castle from the departing British military. These posts were temporarily garrisoned by Michael Brennan's 1st Western Division (Clare and south Galway), which was pro-Treaty. Brennan was in charge and his men also took over five city police barracks from the RIC. The date was 23 February. Brennan was joined by men from Malone's brigade (which was by no means unanimous in its support of Malone and his proclamation).

Brennan's orders were to hold the posts until the rank and file and such senior officers in Limerick as remained loyal to GHQ could be organized to occupy them. On Sunday, 5 March, Captain Sean Hurley, the Mid-Limerick Brigade Quartermaster, paraded pro-Treaty members of the various companies in Limerick with a view to getting a maintenance party to relieve the 1st Western men and allow them to return to their own divisional area. Hurley's troops were unarmed. They were surprised and surrounded by armed anti-Treaty forces, including units brought in from Cork, Tipperary and elsewhere at the request of O'Malley. Hurley was arrested and marched off to prison.

The garrison troops were quickly confronted by a large anti-Treaty force mobilized by O'Malley and under his personal command. They must evacuate the posts and clear out of the city, he demanded, otherwise he would attack. He had at his disposal, in addition to local men, troops drawn from many parts; some from western divisions, some from Cork and Tipperary. He had them installed in the Glentworth, Royal George and other hotels, in a wing of the mental hospital, in the custom house and the city and county courthouses. Senior officers who had come in to support him included Tom Barry, 1st Southern Division; Michael Kilroy, OC 5th Western Division; Sean Moylan, OC Cork No 4 Brigade; Tom Hales, OC Cork No 3, and Seamus Robinson, OC Tipperary No 3. Pro-Treaty reinforcements arrived on the scene, including 150 men from east Limerick under Major-General Donncadh O'Hannigan. In all, about 700 armed men from each side faced one another. A third factor was the British, who still had troops in two city posts from which they sent out patrols in armoured cars.

The ultimatum was ignored by Brennan and the GHQ officers. They intended to stay, and the confrontation must erupt into civil war if O'Malley attacked them. He was acting completely on his own, independently not only of Dáil Éireann and GHQ, but of the anti-Treaty Military Council that he had helped to set up in Dublin. The potentially explosive situation remained primed over four days while the anxious citizens of Limerick held their breath and hoped there would be no slaughter in their streets. In vain, the Mayor, Alderman Stephen O'Mara, and others sought a peaceful solution.

Such was the situation when Liam Lynch was called to GHQ in Beggars' Bush barracks and told that he must persuade O'Malley to withdraw his troops from the buildings they had occupied in Limerick if hostilities were to be averted. Accompanied by Oscar Traynor he went immediately to Limerick. Neither of these anti-Treaty officers had authority over O'Malley, but their mission was at the behest of GHQ in Beggars' Bush.

Lynch secured an amicable settlement that was signed in the presence of Mulcahy as Dáil Minister for Defence and Collins as Chairman of the Provisional Government. There are conflicting accounts of the terms. One must accept Lynch's version as given in a letter to the *Irish Independent* dated 27 April 1922. In it he stated that the settlement provided for the handing over of the four [sic] RIC barracks to the charge of the Limerick Corporation and the installation of a small maintenance party — responsible to himself — in the two military barracks. 'It was,' he wrote, 'a happy consummation for me to see about 700 armed troops on each side who were about to engage in mortal combat, eventually leave Limerick as comrades.' [22]

The Limerick episode demonstrated the readiness of the anti-Treaty IRA to attack positions held by troops loyal to GHQ on the order of a mutinous divisional commander. The fact that O'Malley was a signatory to the request for an army convention must have set alarm bells ringing in Dáil Éireann.

Though the Dáil Cabinet had, on 27 February, given sanction for the holding of the convention, it was cancelled on 15 March by Richard Mulcahy, acting on the unanimous decision of the Dáil Cabinet. He told the Cabinet that if the convention were held he could not guarantee that 'there would not be set up a body regarding itself as a military government not responsible to the people'.[23] On the following day, an order banning the convention was signed by Arthur Griffith as President of Dáil Éireann. On 23 March, Mulcahy, in a letter to O'Duffy, warned that any officer or man who attended the convention would sever his connection with the pro-Treaty IRA.[24]

The previous day, Rory O'Connor had given an interview to the press in the course of which he claimed to speak for eighty per cent of the IRA members who were against the Treaty. In reply to a question, he said there was then no Government in Ireland to which they gave allegiance. 'In effect,' he told the press, 'the holding of the convention means that we repudiate the Dáil.' He was then asked if it could be taken that there was going to be military dictatorship. 'You can take it that way if you like,' he replied.[25]

The Provisional Government did not attempt to prevent the holding of the convention, which assembled in the Mansion House, Dublin, on 26 March. It was attended by delegates from all parts of the country, but the Mulcahy letter ensured that the attendance included very few delegates of pro-Treaty persuasion. The attitude of the pro-Treaty side of the IRA was that they must remain the army of whatever future government was elected by the Irish people, whereas the convention elected a temporary Executive of sixteen military leaders to constitute the sole authority of the IRA.[26] This was the IRA split of 1922. In effect, the anti-Treaty side, which claimed the allegiance of more than seventy per cent of the army, had broken with any kind of democratic governmental authority. In such a situation, the maintenance of IRA unity was not possible.

The Executive lost no time in issuing a statement declaring that the Minister for Defence and his Chief of Staff no longer exercised control over the IRA. The statement also called for an end to recruitment for the Provisional Government Army and for the new national police force called the Civic Guard (later the Gárda Síochána).

Meanwhile de Valera had formed Cumann na Poblachta, a new republican party, with himself as president, although it was not long since he had been seeking a way out of what he saw as the 'the straitjacket of the republic'.[27] In mid-March 1922, in the course of a series of anti-Treaty speeches delivered to public meetings at Dungarvan, Carrick-on-Suir, Thurles and Killarney in the presence of armed men, he fired highly inflammatory verbal salvos into what was already a dangerously explosive atmosphere.

At Dungarvan on 16 March, he said he was 'against the Treaty because it bars the way to independence with the blood of fellow Irishmen. It is only by civil war after this that they can get their independence ...' (*Irish Independent*, 17 March 1922).

At Carrick-on-Suir on Saint Patrick's Day, he said that 'if the Treaty is not rejected, perhaps it is over the bodies of the young men I see around me this day that the fight for Irish freedom may be fought ...' (*Irish Independent*, 18 March 1922).

On the same day at Thurles, he said: 'If they [the people] accept the Treaty and if the Volunteers of the future try to complete the work the Volunteers of the last four years have been attempting, they will have to complete it, not over the bodies of foreign soldiers, but over the dead bodies of their own countrymen. They will have to wade through Irish blood, through the blood of the soldiers of the Irish Government and through, perhaps, the blood of some members of the Government to get Irish freedom.' (*Irish Independent*, 18 March 1922).

Resuming his campaign against the Treaty on 19 March, he said at Killarney: 'Therefore, in future, in order to achieve freedom, if our Volunteers continue, and I hope they will continue until the goal is reached — and if we continue on that movement which was begun when the Volunteers were started, and we suppose this Treaty is ratified by your votes, then these men, in order to achieve freedom, will have, as I said yesterday, to march over the bodies of their own brothers. They will have to wade through Irish blood ...' (*Irish Independent*, 20 March 1922).[28]

De Valera did not disclaim the foregoing pronouncements, but he frequently and resentfully insisted that his 'plain meaning' was deliberately and maliciously misrepresented as incitement to civil war by villainous editorials which the *Irish Independent* published simultaneously with the reports of his speeches. The awful warnings were prophecies of what he believed would happen if the Treaty were ratified, he explained, and were not incitements to civil war. 'This a child might understand,' he wrote of the quoted passages from his Thurles speech in a letter published by the *Irish Independent* on 23 March 1922.

In truth, the use of such words was entirely irresponsible in the prevailing circumstances. In Cork, Collins called the speeches 'the language of madness'. Their really dangerous aspect was the message they conveyed to thousands of anti-Treaty IRA men at a time when the country was in a highly volatile state. In effect, they were warning the electorate that a vote for the Treaty was a vote for civil war.

On coming to power ten years later and working the Treaty as a stepping-stone towards complete independence (what Collins had asked him to do in 1922), de Valera admitted having underestimated the freedom permitted under its articles[29] and by subsequent changes in British legislation. Kevin O'Higgins and Patrick McGilligan, as Free State Ministers for Foreign Affairs, had each played a formidable part in bringing about the changes. The removal of the Governor-General and the oath of allegiance to the Crown (main grounds for opposition to the Treaty), as well as recovery of the Treaty ports, were stepping-stones crossed by de Valera in the thirties. Another step was the inauguration of the Republic of Ireland on 18 April 1949 and the repeal of the External Relations Act of 1936 by John A. Costello's Coalition Government.[30]

Despite their military and political differences, which rapidly became more acute immediately after the convention on 26 March, important leaders on both sides of the Treaty divide strove earnestly to restore IRA unity. There were even joint discussions about military aid to the stricken nationalists in Belfast, Derry and elsewhere in the North, who were being killed and wounded by the Special Constabulary; armed Orange mobs also drove tens of thousands of Catholics from their homes and work places. But a background of provocative military activity by anti-Treaty forces in Dublin and up and down the provinces made a mockery of peace talks in the 'South'. In fact, a divisive bitterness was tearing the twenty-six counties apart and driving the IRA more and more into two mutually hostile camps. The defiance of Dáil Éireann (in which de Valera and his followers sat on the Opposition benches) and Army GHQ by the mutinous anti-Treaty officers and their followers had led to open contempt of law and authority in any shape or form over wide areas. Discipline was lax. Men seemed to be spoiling for fight in the cause of the republic. There was talk of civil war. Every town and village had its quota of inflammable material. Rival forces occupied different military posts in the same locality.

There was widespread seizure of arms issued to Provisional Government troops engaged in taking over garrisons from the departing British. In some cases these troops went over with their arms and joined the anti-Treaty side. Stored arms belonging to the RIC were seized. British armouries were raided. The most sensational episode of this kind occurred on 29 March 1922 when units of Cork No 1 Brigade of the

1st Southern Division (anti-Treaty), under the direction of Brigade Commandant Sean O'Hegarty, captured the British Admiralty vessel *Upnor* at sea. The 700-ton *Upnor* was on a direct course for Portsmouth. She had sailed from Haulbowline Island with a cargo of naval arms and ammunition. Pursued and overtaken by the Cork No 1 men in a commandeered tug, *Warrior*, she was boarded and her captain, taken completely by surprise, was forced to turn about at gun point and make for Ballycotton Bay, about ten miles east of Cork Harbour. At the quayside her entire cargo was off-loaded on to a waiting fleet of lorries and private cars. The haul is said by one writer to have consisted of 1,500 rifles, fifty-five Lewis guns, six Maxim guns, three Vickers machine-guns, half a million rounds of .303 ammunition, 1,000 revolvers and 1,000 .455 automatic pistols with ammunition for both, 3,000 hand grenades and a quantity of rifle-grenade throwers.[31] It was a brilliant coup of the greatest value to the anti-Treaty side of the IRA. It was also an episode of grave concern to Michael Collins; the *Upnor* had no escort, and he wondered why the British had suddenly become so careless with their war materials. The 1st Southern had, in November 1921, received some 200 rifles and 10,000 rounds of ammunition, run from Hamburg to an island off Cheekpoint, County Waterford, by Charlie McGuinness of Derry, an adventurous seafaring character whose exploits included the sensational rescue of Commandant Frank Carty from Derry jail where Carty was under sentence of death. A much larger load of munitions that he ran from Bremen to Ring pier, near Dungarvan, in April 1922, was conveyed overland to the IRA divisions north of the border.

The anti-Treaty army convention resumed at the Mansion House on 9 April and adopted a new constitution in the framing of which the oath of allegiance to the Irish Republic and the Government of the Irish Republic (Dáil Éireann), taken by all Volunteers in the autumn of 1920 was altered by the deletion of the pledge of allegiance to Dáil Éireann as the Government of the Republic. The Executive of sixteen members, as appointed temporarily on 26 March, was approved, and under the new constitution their forces were to be at the disposal of an established Republican Government that would replace the Provisional Government. There was talk of eliminating all four governments then claiming some authority in Ireland — the Provisional, Dáil Éireann, the British and the Northern Ireland — without a word as to how this might be accomplished. In the event, what the discussions boiled down to, as an issue to be decided by the Executive, was whether or not the IRA should attempt, by force, to prevent the holding of a general election in the twenty-six counties on the issue of the Treaty. This was considered by the Executive on the following day. (In that strange era of our advance towards the ultimate freedom that is yet to come, the people were told they had no right to do wrong.)[32]

On the 14th, Liam Mellows, as secretary of that body, sent a letter to the secretary of Dáil Éireann, setting out six conditions on which the Executive would agree to 'reunification of the IRA'. These included an undertaking to disband the Civic Guard, to uphold 'the existing republic' and maintain the army as the IRA under the control of an elected independent executive, with all the army's financial liabilities met by the Dáil; and an agreement that 'no election on the issue at present before the country [the Treaty] be held while the threat of war with England exists'. The letter, and copies sent to all Dáil Éireann deputies on 25 April, met with no response.

The Executive appointed Liam Lynch to be Chief of Staff of their forces. They also appointed an Army Council of seven, which included Liam Lynch, Rory O'Connor, Liam Mellows and Joe McKelvey, and possibly Ernie O'Malley, Seamus Robinson and Peadar O'Donnell.[33]

TOWARDS CIVIL WAR

Anti-Treaty troops led by their Chief of Staff, General Liam Lynch, Rory O'Connor, Liam Mellows and Ernie O'Malley, commenced occupying public buildings in Dublin. They occupied the Four Courts on 14 April and established their headquarters there. The Kildare Street Club, the Ballast Office and Lever Brothers' premises in Essex Street, the Masonic

Hall in Molesworth Street and Kilmainham jail were taken over and garrisoned on succeeding days. Such occupation was of no military value and no military plan had been formulated. In fact, members of the Executive were soon in disagreement about policy, and individual anti-Treaty officers were acting without authority or control. Outside the Four Courts, Oscar Traynor had less authority over his brigade than was exercised by Rory O'Connor and Liam Mellows from inside. We learn from Dorothy Macardle that, also from inside the Courts, 'Ernie O'Malley, Andrew McDonnell [OC South Dublin Brigade], Sean MacBride and other enterprising young commandants carried out independent activities from time to time.' [34] These and other operations, carried out in the name of the republic, did not always have the authority of General Lynch and, as often as not, were engaged in without his knowledge. [35] Cathal Brugha vainly opposed the 'independent activities' as being provocative of fratricidal strife. [36]

Roof snipers became active against barracks occupied by Provisional Government troops in Dublin, notably Beggars' Bush. Armed clashes were taking place elsewhere in the country. Anti-Treaty troops moved from Tipperary against the Provisional Government garrison in Kilkenny city, but were repulsed. Strenuous efforts were being made to prevent the recruitment and expansion of the Government's armed forces and the Civic Guard.

Local anti-Treaty commandants up and down the country were carrying on a campaign to obstruct and prevent any explanation of the Treaty or interpretation of its articles through the medium of public meetings, then a most important means of communicating with the people. On 13 March, shots were fired in an unsuccessful attempt to stampede a huge crowd which had assembled in Cork to hear Michael Collins speak on the Treaty. At Charleville a few days later, a pro-Treaty meeting was dispersed by rifle-fire. Liam Pilkington, entirely on his own initiative, concentrated a large force of anti-Treaty troops in Sligo town to enforce his much publicized proclamation forbidding the public meeting scheduled to be addressed in the town by President Griffith on 16 April. He was outwitted and outmanoeuvered by Sean MacEoin's handling of a strong body of Free State trooops supported by an armoured car, and the attempt to prevent the meeting was a fiasco. Guarded by MacEoin, Griffith and others spoke from a lorry and there was a big turnout to hear them.

Michael Collins's public meetings advertised for Killarney on Saturday, 22 April, and for Tralee on the following day were prohibited by proclamations of Brigadier John Joe Rice (Killarney) and Brigadier Humphrey Murphy (Tralee). Collins was accompanied to Killarney by Sean MacEoin, Fionan Lynch, Padraig O'Keeffe and an army escort of ten men under Commandant Joe Dolan. Rice's attempt to make his proclamation effective by force of arms was brushed aside by MacEoin and Dolan. He also had railway gates locked and chained and had roads blocked for miles around Killarney. His men burned the speakers' platform. Collins and his party smashed their way through the railway gates and he and others spoke from a brake in the grounds of the Franciscan Friary, where a most successful meeting was held. Murphy had notices published in Tralee giving 'the invaders' twelve hours to leave the town. The 'invaders' were Collins and his party with their escort and twenty-four additional pro-Treaty troops under Commandant Dinny Galvin from Knocknagoshel who were there to ensure freedom of speech. The troops were not needed. On Sunday morning, Murphy made it his business to meet MacEoin on the common ground of membership of the Irish Republican Brotherhood. (The IRB was a secret organization, set up in 1858 by veterans of the Young Ireland movement of 1848, whose oath gave allegiance to the 'Irish Republic'.) They met without escorts and the outcome was an agreement and a joint statement, signed by both. The public meeting would proceed. Murphy's troops would be confined to Ballymullen barracks and the 'invaders' to their posts in the Central Technical School and the Central Hotel in Denny Street, from one o'clock that day. A large crowd gathered to welcome Michael Collins to their predominantly anti-Treaty town and hear him speak from a platform in Denny Street. There was some heckling, which was challenged by Eamon Horan, of whom more later. This apart, it was an orderly and successful meeting and Collins spoke to an attentive audience.

The campaign against the right of public meeting and free speech was a strange feature of opposition to the Treaty by forces who claimed to be 'standing by the republic' and dedicated to the cause of Irish freedom. It meant that free elections on the issue of the Treaty were not possible.

By removing their forces from Dáil Éireann control the Executive had cut them off from financial and any other form of Government support. Not surprisingly, the Minister for Defence refused to authorize payment of their debts, including debts incurred by them prior to the convention of 26 March. On 12 April, the Executive responded with a decision to finance their forces by raids on the official bank of the Provisional Government, the Bank of Ireland. Branches of the bank throughout the country were raided on 1 May and large sums of money were seized at gunpoint; Piaras Beaslai put the total amount at £275,000.[37] The laconic comment by Ernie O'Malley was that Griffith and Mulcahy could compensate the bank.[38]

The slide towards anarchy had accelerated. There was no shortage of guns or of men to brandish them in raids on banks and post-offices and in the commandeering of 'goods for the troops' from traders, which events were of daily occurrence in the twenty-six counties. Money was seized from 323 post-offices in the three weeks from 29 March to 19 April. Forty consignments of goods were seized from the Dublin and South Eastern Railway between 23 March and 22 April, though in only thirty cases was the seizure stated to be 'by order IRA'.[39] It was never known for certain whether a raid was an official action carried out by the Executive forces or a private enterprise job by criminals taking advantage of the fact that there was no established authority in the country. The state of lawlessness reached rock bottom with the intervention of armed men in land disputes and other local quarrels. Parts of the south and west were seething with agrarian unrest. Cleeves threatened to close all their twelve creameries in Munster towns unless the workers accepted a wage reduction. On 13 May, the workers seized the creameries and declared soviets. Red flags were hoisted over the plants and other establishments in Cork, Limerick and Tipperary.

All efforts to find a basis for IRA unity seemed doomed. The IRB had failed in the attempt. Intervention by the Archbishop of Dublin, the Lord Mayor and the Labour Party had achieved nothing. Liam Lynch saw no point in continuing IRB meetings about unity unless 'the other side' would guarantee to produce a republican constitution within two days.[40] The republic would have to be maintained and the Free State would not be allowed to come into existence, 'no matter what sacrifice may be necessary to prevent it'.[41] Such was the keynote of opposition to the Treaty and it would brook no argument.

That was the situation on 29 April, and to Florence O'Donoghue it looked as if the last hope of peace had vanished. Since the early months of the year he had taken a leading part in the IRB attempts at bridging 'the deep but narrow chasm' which separated the opposing sides of the IRA. Dan Breen, just back from America, was sick at heart. It was clear to him that civil war might break out at any moment. 'War was in the air. All through the night the noise of gunfire could be heard [in Dublin]: armoured cars were patrolling the streets.'[42] Disillusioned by the terms of the Treaty, to which he was bitterly antagonistic, Breen had emigrated to America. His return to Ireland was at the request of Liam Lynch.[43] In a last desperate effort to avert civil war he sought out high ranking officers of 'the old fighting crowd' who 'were now on opposite sides'. He brought them together and presided over their peace conferences.

The officers reached agreement on the basis of acceptance of the Treaty and 'of the fact — admitted by all sides — that the majority of the people of Ireland are willing to accept the Treaty'.[44] They pleaded for an agreed election with view to the formation of a coalition government which would have the confidence of the whole country. Their views were put forward in a manifesto signed by ten senior officers, five from each side, and published on 1 May.

The signatories were Dan Breen; Tom Hales, OC Cork No 3 Brigade; Humphrey Murphy, OC Kerry No 1 Brigade; Florence O'Donoghue, Adjutant 1st Southern Division; Sean O'Hegarty, OC Cork No 1 Brigade; Sean Boylan, OC 1st Eastern Division; Richard Mulcahy, Minister for Defence; Eoin

O'Duffy, Chief of Staff; Gearoid O'Sullivan, Adjutant-General, and Michael Collins, Chairman of the Provisional Government. The first five signatories belonged to the anti-Treaty forces and, of these, Hales, O'Donoghue and O'Hegarty were members of the Executive. Sean Moylan, OC Cork No 4 Brigade, was the only officer present who refused to sign.[45]

The reaction of the Executive was predictable. In a statement issued from the Four Courts, the Army Council declared that any agreement upon which the army could be united must be based upon the 'maintenance of the republic'. Deals between individual soldiers could 'only intensify existing disunion.'[46] To the editor of *The Plain People*, an anti-Treaty journal, Dan Breen was a Judas.

Casualties from clashes between anti-Treaty and Provisional Government forces had resulted in eight dead and forty-nine wounded. This was in a period when according to anti-Treaty sources the Civil War had not yet begun. Thus far, losses were light but the menace was heavy. There was urgent need for a truce. An immediate cessation of hostilities was agreed, with effect from four o'clock in the afternoon of 4 May. Under its terms, buildings in Dublin (other than the Four Courts) occupied by anti-Treaty forces were to be evacuated; raids, seizure of cars and commandeering of revenues were to cease. There would be a release of prisoners. It was hoped that in the atmosphere of truce IRA and Dáil committees seeking an acceptable basis for unity would find some means of halting the mad rush towards disaster. Collins warned that if the effort by the Dáil committee failed there would be no other peace conference, and the Government would have to take 'strong action to restore order in the country'.[47] Next day, 16 May, the Dáil committee reported failure.

In what he has described as a last desperate effort to avoid outright civil war and to end the chaos and anarchy that had brought the twenty-six counties to the brink of ruin, Collins, on 18 May, began discussions with de Valera on a proposal for an agreed election with a view to the formation of a coalition government.[48] These discussions were at the request of Dáil Éireann. The genesis of the proposal was the manifesto first published in the evening papers of 1 May over the signatures of the ten senior officers. The officers' proposal was based on acceptance of the Treaty. De Valera made his position absolutely clear in the Dáil on the 17th. He would confer with Collins on the understanding that he and the deputies for whom he spoke were not committed to the Treaty, and that 'the people should not be asked to commit themselves to the Treaty'.[49] On 20 May, both leaders signed a general election pact. It would be a rigged election and would have the effect of postponing a direct vote by the people on acceptance or rejection of the Treaty.

The essence of the pact was that there would be a Sinn Féin Dáil and Government, in which each side of the Treaty divide would have representation roughly proportionate to its membership in the old Dáil. To maintain the proportion, the agreed number of candidates to be put forward as a National Sinn Féin Coalition Panel was fixed at sixty-six pro-Treaty and fifty-eight anti-Treaty. A coalition government would be formed after the election. There would be a President elected by the Dáil, a Minister for Defence representing the IRA (both sides) and nine other Ministers. Collins agreed, 'with the approval of the Government', that the anti-Treaty side would hold four of the nine other offices. Allocation of the Ministries would be a function of the President. The pact was approved by Dáil Éireann with one dissentient, and subsequently by the Sinn Féin Ard Fheis on 23 May.

De Valera had driven a hard bargain and scored a major tactical victory. The last thing he wanted was an election on the Treaty. Collins was, in his own words, 'severely criticized' by Government colleagues for having given away so much of the pro-Treaty position. But he had secured the significant proviso that 'every and any interest' was at liberty to contest the election with the coalition candidates and this gave some safeguard to the electoral rights of the people. Nevertheless, the pact was a gross violation of the principles of democracy.

The pact alarmed the British and led to an immediate crisis in Anglo-Irish affairs. They could not see the Treaty being upheld by a government that included de Valera and his political followers. The evacuation of their troops was suspended, as was the transfer of arms and military stores to the Provisional Government. Griffith and Collins were summoned to London. The whole Anglo-Irish settlement hung in the balance.

The pact had angered Griffith, and it was with reluctance that he agreed to recommend it to the Dáil. Yet it was mainly through him that the crisis was resolved. He assured the British ministers that he and his colleagues stood firmly by the Treaty. But he also told them that the pact was for the Irish people to settle, and for them alone; it was not the concern of the British and would not prevent the Treaty from being put into operation.

The senior anti-Treaty officers, arguing amongst themselves and disagreeing, never seem to have planned for an outcome which many regarded as inevitable. Sean O'Hegarty, Florence O'Donoghue and Tom Hales had resigned from the Executive on the issue of an attempt to prevent forcibly the holding of the general election.[50] They were replaced by Tom Barry, Pat Whelan and Tom Derrig. Meanwhile, representatives of the two sides of the IRA were proceeding with their negotiations for reconciliation. When a crisis developed on 7 June, Richard Mulcahy and Liam Lynch came together in yet another effort to avert civil war. Agreement was reached between them on proposals that would have given the anti-Treaty side enormous influence over a reunited IRA, which would have the right to hold periodic conventions. Initially, at any rate, the anti-Treaty side would have five representatives on an Army Council of eight members who, by majority vote, would control the appointment of the Minister for Defence and the Chief of Staff. Furthermore, under a curious arrangement, the anti-Treaty side would hold three of the five principal posts on the GHQ. The IRA would be under the control of a parliament and a coalition government elected in accordance with the Collins-de Valera pact.[51]

The settlement proposals were received with dismay by most members of the Government and by many senior pro-Treaty officers. Nevertheless, they were rejected by the Executive. When that body met on 14 June only Liam Lynch, Liam Deasy and Sean Moylan of its sixteen members were in favour of the proposals as set out for them by Mulcahy two days previously.[52] Sean MacBride, anti-Treaty Assistant Director of Organization but not a member of the Executive, held that acceptance would put the IRA entirely under the control of the Provisional Government. He saw clearly that there was 'a very big split' in the Executive on 'an absolutely fundamental decision of policy'.[53]

Also, at their 14 June meeting, the Executive resolved to instruct their officers deputed to meet 'the Beggars' Bush officers' that negotiation for army unification must cease. They decided to take whatever action was necessary to 'maintain the republic against British aggression', but agreed that no offensive would be taken by their troops against the Beggars' Bush forces. A copy of the resolution was handed to Mulcahy by Rory O'Connor and Ernie O'Malley on the same day.[54]

To the British, the Free State Constitution, not the pact, was the crucial factor, and on 1 June Lloyd George's Cabinet emphatically rejected the draft constitution that Griffith brought over to London.

A republic in disguise was how Lloyd George himself described it, indeed an accurate description of what Collins tried to have carried through. The British remained 'unalterably opposed' to any proposal of the sort. Strenuous and protracted argument ended with the Irish representatives avoiding a break by accepting that the Constitution must be within the framework of the Treaty. As such, it had to be rejected by de Valera, which meant that the pact was at an end. In fact, it was already a dead letter before Collins, speaking in Cork on 14 June, urged the people to vote for the candidates they thought best. Polling day was the 16th. The Constitution was published in the press of that morning.

Other interests had asserted their right to contest the election in opposition to the Sinn Féin panel candidates. When the results were announced on 24 June it was found that pro-Treaty Sinn Féin had won 58 of the 128 seats. Anti-Treaty Sinn Féin had won only 35. More significant, however, was the election of 31 candidates representing other interests that were prepared to work the Treaty: seventeen Labour, seven

Farmers and seven Independents (besides four representatives of Dublin University returned unopposed). Of the 620,283 votes cast, the 'other interests' between them received 247,226, some thousands more than pro-Treaty Sinn Féin (239,193) and almost double anti-Treaty Sinn Féin (133,864). Clearly, forty per cent of the people who voted were disenchanted with both sides of Sinn Féin, but they supported the Treaty, not least because it appeared to offer the best prospect of peace and an early return to normal living. It is reasonable to say that, in the overall, the result of the election was an emphatic acceptance of the Treaty, and that the Collins–de Valera pact had ensured an orderly election, despite intimidation by anti-Treaty extremists attempting to prevent non-pact candidates from standing in some constituencies.

Diehard Sinn Féin never did recognize the new Dáil (the third) as Dáil Éireann.

Serious disagreement arose at the army convention on 18 June when the delegates who had constituted the conventions of 26 March and 9 April reassembled in Dublin. 'At Liam Lynch's pressing request', Florence O'Donoghue moved the adoption of the army reunification proposals as set out by Mulcahy and rejected by the Executive on 14 June.[55] Lynch and the delegates, and the two members of the Executive who shared his views, believed that the proposals should be adopted by the convention as the only remaining hope of averting civil war. O'Donoghue has recorded that the motion was debated in 'an atmosphere of disillusion and anger' created by the publication, two days previously, of a constitution 'subject to the terms of the Treaty', and by what the delegates held to be Collins's repudiation of the election pact with de Valera.[56] After the debate had proceeded for some time, Tom Barry, who was totally opposed to the proposals, came to his feet and moved that instead of discussing them any further the convention should consider a motion to resume the war against the British forces in Ireland.[57] The Provisional Government forces in Beggars' Bush or elsewhere in Ireland were not to be attacked. At the time, British military only occupied posts in Dublin and the Six Counties. Barry's motion was opposed by Liam Lynch, by

Cathal Brugha, by virtually the entire 1st Southern delegation and by many other delegates. Rory O'Connor and Liam Mellows spoke in favour of it.

On a show of hands, Barry's motion appeared to have been carried by a couple of votes. This was challenged. A poll was demanded with the result that 103 voted for the motion and 118 against, whereupon the delegates departed in angry disagreement.[58] Rory O'Connor and his followers of the war faction went to the Four Courts, there to depose Liam Lynch as Chief of Staff and appoint Joe McKelvey in his stead. Lynch and the majority retired to the Clarence Hotel, which became a headquarters in opposition to the Four Courts, both in opposition to the headquarters of the Government forces in Beggars' Bush, and all three calling themselves the IRA.

CIVIL WAR

Since 25 June, conciliation talks had been taking place between the anti-Treaty IRA in the Clarence Hotel and the anti-Treaty IRA occupying the Four Courts. They were trying to devise a policy on which they could agree and thus heal the differences that had split the delegates at their convention on the 18th. Accord was achieved and Liam Lynch was reinstated as Chief of Staff. At his Clarence Hotel headquarters he awoke in the early dawn of Wednesday, 28 June 1922, to the sound of the bombardment of the Courts by Provisional Government forces. Held prisoner inside the barricaded buildings was Lieutenant-General J.J. (Ginger) O'Connell, Deputy Assistant Chief of Staff of the Government Army. Unarmed and unattended, he had been kidnapped by Four Courts officers in retaliation for the arrest of Leo Henderson, one of their officers, by Government troops. The anti-Treatyites in the Courts had announced their intention to hold him as a prisoner until Henderson was released. They had expected the situation to be resolved by an exchange of the prisoners.

The kidnap of O'Connell was a crucial link in the chain of events that immediately preceded the attack on the Courts, which was inevitable in any event. Its occupation was a direct challenge that could not be ignored by the Provisional

Government. Another link in the chain was the shooting dead of Field Marshal Sir Henry Wilson outside his own house in London, on 22 June, by Commandant Reginald Dunne, OC London Battalion IRA, and Volunteer Joseph O'Sullivan, both of whom were captured and subsequently hanged. It is probable that the execution of the fanatically anti-Irish Field-Marshal, a County Longford man, was ordered by Collins.

Mistakenly, the British laid responsibility for the shooting of Wilson at the door of the anti-Treaty leadership in the Four Courts. Rory O'Connor, from the Courts, denied all knowledge of it. Griffith condemned it. De Valera denounced it. The British attitude was uncompromising. The British Government 'shall regard the Treaty as having been formally violated,' Churchill told the House of Commons on the 26th, and they would resume 'full liberty of action' unless the occupation of the Four Courts was brought to a speedy end by the Provisional Government. As it happened, his speech almost caused a reversal of the decision to attack the Courts. 'When O'Connell was kidnapped we did decide to move and the order was given,' Griffith told the historian P.S. O'Hegarty on the second day of the Four Courts fighting. 'Then came Churchill's speech, and we wavered ... Some of us wanted to cancel it. But we said that we had either to go on or to abdicate, and finally we went on.'[59] It was a unanimous decision, taken at a joint meeting of the Dáil Cabinet and the Provisional Government.

Within hours of the first boom from the only piece of artillery used in the attack, Liam Lynch sent a message to the besieged Four Courts garrison telling them that he was going to rouse the country in defence of the republic.[60] He held a meeting of all available anti-Treaty senior officers in the Clarence Hotel, after which a proclamation was issued over the names of all sixteen members of the Army Executive: 'Fellow citizens of the Irish Republic. At the dictation of our hereditary enemy our rightful cause is being treacherously assailed by recreant Irishmen ... Gallant soldiers of the Irish Republic stand vigorously in its defence ... The sacred spirits of the Illustrious Dead are with us in this great struggle ... "Death before Dishonour" ... We, therefore, appeal to all citizens ... to rally to the support of the Republic. . .' [61]

Oscar Traynor immediately took over Barry's Hotel in Great Denmark Street, Dublin, as an anti-Treaty mobilization centre. He had troops posted in buildings in Parnell Square and Capel Street, and in a block of buildings in Sackville Street, which included the Gresham and Hammam Hotels. The Rotunda was also occupied by his troops. He set up his headquarters in the Hammam, there to await the arrival of ten thousand troops from the provinces.[62] No troops came.

De Valera, in a public statement, declared that those who were being attacked in the Four Courts were 'the best and bravest of our nation'. This done, he reported at the 3rd Battalion Dublin Brigade mobilization centre and was attached to the battalion's headquarters staff. In this way he entered into a period of oblivion, where he remained without influence or authority to change the course of events. For practical purposes, control as well as leadership of the anti-Treaty forces gradually passed to Liam Lynch.

Cathal Brugha reported to Traynor for war duty and became a commandant in the Dublin Brigade. Eight days later he fell mortally wounded in Thomas's Lane, at the rear of the Gresham Hotel, having refused to surrender, as once before in 1916.

The occupation of buildings in Dublin was 1916 military thinking in terms of national defiance, which amounted to nothing in anti-Treaty military achievement. Anti-Treaty IRA members have maintained down through the years that the attack on their military headquarters was the cause and the beginning of the Civil War. In reality, it was the Provisional Government's assertion of authority in a country torn by strife and lawlessness. It was a clear-cut decision of military initiative from which the anti-Treaty cause never recovered.

The crisis of the Four Courts attack ended the romantic days enjoyed by so many since the signing of the Anglo-Irish Truce. The guns were out again in deadly earnest and the awesome task of providing a military defence of the new state devolved on the Army Council under the Provisional Government: Richard Mulcahy, Chief of Staff and Minister for Defence; Michael Collins, Director of Intelligence and Minister for Finance; Eoin O'Duffy, Assistant Chief of Staff;

Gearoid O'Sullivan, Adjutant-General; Sean MacMahon, Quartermaster-General, and J.J. O'Connell, Deputy Assistant Chief of Staff. These were the senior GHQ staff of the Irish Republican Army who had sided with the Treaty.

The Four Courts fell, as did Oscar Traynor's posts in Sackville Street and elsewhere in Dublin, with nothing achieved except death and enormous destruction of property.[63] It was suicidal to attempt to fight the Provisional Government by merely occupying buildings in Dublin. The total failure of Traynor's Dublin Brigade (or whatever experienced fighting elements of it supported him) to provide support for the besieged Four Courts garrison indicated the lack of any kind of military plan on the part of those who constituted themselves the republican side of the IRA. There was no cohesion, no communication in a military sense, no prepared knowledge of who was where and how mobilization could be effected. It was total failure in every sense, regardless of whatever might be said about noble sacrifice.

The influence of the Dublin IRA Active Service Unit at that juncture of divided loyalties cannot be underestimated. The ASU went Free State almost totally, its loyalty given to Michael Collins as head of the Provisional Government, and not to Oscar Traynor's Dublin Brigade. It is not unreasonable to suggest that a body of some fifty men of the calibre of the ASU and the Squad (joined since May 1921 to form the Guard) could have turned the whole concept of the Civil War had its loyalty been given elsewhere. The ASU would have been capable of seizing and imprisoning the top personnel of the Provisional Government and its Army GHQ, thereby stultifying at once the pro-Treaty direction of military and civil affairs. Instead, as the Dublin Guard, the ASU provided the first unit of the Free State Army.

After the Four Courts surrender (the garrison held out for two and a half days), Ernie O'Malley, who was a formidable leader and fighting officer, escaped and made his way to the Wicklow mountains. He endeavoured to rally the available anti-Treaty units for an attack on the Government posts in Dublin, but they proved to be disastrously few, and eventually, on receiving word from Traynor that all was over in the capital, he abandoned a thought that had never matured as a plan and headed south via Wexford.

Later on the morning of 28 June, Liam Lynch, isolated from his Southern Divisions and without any plan to meet emergencies, tried to make his way by train from Dublin to Mallow. He was arrested when on his way to Kingsbridge railway station and brought before Eoin O'Duffy, to whom, according to Dorothy Macardle, he stated that he 'reserved his decision' about taking part in the fighting.[64] He and Liam Deasy and Sean Culhane, who were with him, were allowed to go free, probably in the belief that he would not take up arms against the Provisional Government. On 30 June, as Chief of Staff, he issued a morale-boosting statement from Mallow. It was addressed 'To all Units', but his words were largely unheeded outside Munster. The other provinces responded in their own way, but in a manner that did not threaten the operations of government forces advancing into midland towns and, at the same time, making contact with their garrisons north of Dublin city and in Athlone, Galway and Donegal, as well as with troops in the training centre at the Curragh.

At that stage, Frank Aiken, OC 4th Northern Division, was not committed to either side and, from his headquarters in Dundalk military barracks, was passionately endeavouring to prevent the spread of war between old comrades. However, he was strongly anti-Treaty and, on 16 July, Provisional Government forces moved against him.

In Belfast, where fighting still continued with much ferocity, the great majority of the IRA under Commandant Roger McCorley, then recovered from grievous wounds, gave loyalty to GHQ, meaning the Provisional Government forces under the command of their headquarters. Until the eve of the attack on the Four Courts, the divided IRA in the south had shared a common policy of encouraging and organizing armed resistance in the Six Counties. Collins and O'Duffy, with the co-operation of Lynch, had been secretly sending arms to the North, using boats across Carlingford Bay and oil tankers to Belfast.

With the outbreak of Civil War in the south, pressure on

the IRA above the border was stepped up dramatically by the Northern Government, using more than 30,000 special constables and the Royal Ulster Constabulary. There were also 7,500 British troops stationed there. Drives and sweeps against the nationalist population resulted in hundreds of arrests. Many were interned on board the prison ship *Argenta* in Belfast Lough. In August, some ninety per cent of the active members of the 2nd and 3rd Northern Divisions who had avoided arrest came south and assembled at the Curragh for training. They were under, respectively, Dan McKenna, later Chief of Staff of the National Army, and Roger McCorley. All were paid out of Dáil funds. Hundreds volunteered for war service with the army of the Provisional Government, as did many more who had crossed the border into County Donegal. Others simply remained neutral for the duration of the war. A detachment of the northern troops from the Curragh under McCorley served in south Kerry.

The weeks that followed the Four Courts surrender were critical on both sides, but it became increasingly clear that the new regular army being raised by the Provisional Government had an enormous advantage through fixed governmental authority and established procedure, together with resources of finance. The Provisional Government had been in existence for almost six months prior to the outbreak of hostilities at the Courts. In that time, despite the toing and froing of opposing political and military heads, it was able to build resources and make emergency plans. It could keep its 'front' busy in talks, arguments and disagreements about maintaining the IRA as the nation's volunteer army, while building and strengthening the new regular army. It had the means of doing what it wished to do, while observing very closely the growing aggressiveness of an opposition which spent its time thinking and talking, without agreeing on what was to be done or how to go about doing it. That was where the line of demarcation lay.

GHQ of the Provisional Government Army could plan and command from its military establishments in Dublin and in the Curragh and Athlone. In the initial stage of the Civil War it was served by an enlisted force of some 4,000 officers and men based in the Dublin barracks of Beggars' Bush, Portobello, Wellington (now Griffith) and Islandbridge.[65] At the outbreak of the Four Courts hostilities, the anti-Treaty military leaders had vastly greater numbers under arms,[66] particularly in the south and parts of the west, but they failed to use them. They failed to position them as a striking force at a time when the Government forces were at their most vulnerable. Their great weakness was their indecision, with the inevitable result that they never, at any time, gained the initiative.

In Dublin on 7 July the Provisional Government issued 'A National Call to Arms'. This was a bold move and it had an immediate response. It was an expression of authority which demonstrated without equivocation that the Provisional Government was prepared to uphold the will of the people as expressed in the general election on 16 June and to restore order in the country. The pro-Treaty army was now officially called the National Army. Recruiting offices were opened in centres that corresponded to the organizational area of the pre-Truce Dublin Brigade IRA as follows: 1st Battalion, King's Inns, Henrietta Street; 2nd Battalion, Amiens Street railway station; 3rd Battalion, Brunswick Street; 4th Battalion, Kilmainham police-station, and 5th Battalion, Swords police-station. So great were the numbers responding to the appeal that within a week additional recruiting offices were opened at the City Hall and at Wellington, Portobello and Beggars' Bush barracks.

During the first fortnight in July, the early enlistments became linked with the increasing numbers of pre-Truce IRA joining by units or as individuals in provincial centres in the north, west, midlands, parts of south Tipperary, Limerick and Clare. In this way a cohesive force of 14,127 officers and other ranks became the early established regular National Army.[67] It was a period of confusion being brought to order by the calm direction of Richard Mulcahy, who had held the post of Chief of Staff of the IRA through the entire period of the War of Independence. The immediate problem at this early stage of the Civil War was the creation of unit organization and control while dealing with the logistics of supply, communication, transport, equipment and training. There was, too, the question of securing sufficient manpower to meet the military commitments that loomed ahead. Individual IRA officers, sympathetic to the Treaty and detached from anti-Treaty forces in the south, warned of the resistance to be expected throughout Munster where the Free State would not be acknowledged by the local IRA units.

At the commencement of the attack on the Four Courts, only two Munster towns were occupied by Provisional Government troops. These were Listowel and Skibbereen. The occupancy did not last. On 30 June, after a great deal of rifle and Lewis-gun fire and minor casualties, the Listowel posts surrendered unconditionally to an anti-Treaty force of 150 men under the command of Humphrey Murphy, the Kerry No 1 Brigadier. Skibbereen was lost to the Government four days later. The surrender of arms and equipment at Listowel (anti-Treaty troops also held positions in the town since 30 April), and in an earlier surrender episode at Lixnaw railway station, south-west of Listowel, was serious, involving the loss of 200 rifles, four Lewis-guns, grenade launchers, a vast quantity of .303 ammunition, uniforms, dormitory and kitchen equipment, one Lancia lorry and two Crossley tenders.[68] Fifty of the Provisional Government garrison of 250 men in Listowel under Tom Kennelly changed sides and joined Murphy's force. It was that kind of war, especially in the early days.

The surrender of the Listowel garrison followed a truce of three hours that was arranged through the efforts of Father Charles (Charlie) Troy, a native of the town and a student at St Patrick's College, Maynooth, at the time. Commandant Kennelly, who was most unhappy at being in battle against former comrades, probably did not need a great deal of persuasion to agree to it. The surrender at Lixnaw was of new recruits, young country boys who had no military training whatsoever. Confronted by a small anti-Treaty force and a demand to surrender, they simply threw away their rifles and headed for the open fields.[69] One of them was scathing in his comment on the Provisional Government forces of those early days in north Kerry. 'Yerra, 'twasn't an army at all,' he recalled in conversation with Mortimer (Murty) O'Sullivan many years later. 'Sure 'twas only a crowd that gathered.'

GHQ at Beggars' Bush believed that the situation of military emergency could be met by the introduction of what was termed a 'Voluntary Levy', better known as the 'Government Reserve Scheme', under which would be formed a regular and reserve force that would reach a combined strength of 30,000 all ranks. In fact, the estimated peak strength of the regular Free State Army at 31 March 1923 was a formidable 3,600 officers and 55,500 COs and privates.[70]

Coincidental with the plans for army expansion, the Government, on 16 July, announced that 'the conduct of the war' was vested in a War Council consisting of three members: General Michael Collins, Commander-in-Chief; General Richard Mulcahy, Minister for Defence and Chief of the General Staff to the Commander-in-Chief, and General Eoin O'Duffy, Assistant Chief of Staff. Additional appointments to the General Staff were: Fionan Lynch, with the rank of Commandant-General; Kevin O'Higgins, Assistant Adjutant-General, with the rank of Commandant-General; Joseph McGrath, Director of Intelligence, with the rank of Major-General, and Diarmuid O'Hegarty, Commandant-General on General Staff.

The National Army was divided into five commands:

South–Western Command, consisting of Clare, Limerick, Kerry, Cork. General Eoin O'Duffy in command, assisted by Commandant-General Fionan Lynch and Commandant-General W.R.E. Murphy.

Western Command, consisting of Midland, 2nd, 3rd & 4th Western Divisions (Longford, Roscommon, Westmeath and areas of Galway, Sligo, Leitrim and Cavan). Major-General Sean MacEoin in command.

Eastern Command, consisting of 4th and 5th Northern Divisions, 1st and 2nd Eastern Divisions, Carlow and South Wexford Brigades. Major-General Emmet Dalton in command.

South Eastern Command, consisting of Kilkenny, Waterford, Tipperary South and Mid. Commandant-General J.T. Prout in command.

Curragh Command, consisting of 3rd Southern Division

with special Curragh area attached. Lieutenant-General J.J. O'Connell in command.

These appointments constituted the field organization required to deal with the military situation at mid-July. Inevitably, time brought about changes, both in personnel and in areas of command, but this was the base line for future action.

It was charged during the Civil War, and later, that the Provisional Government authorities accepted into army service men who had served with the British forces. This is true, of course, and such men were entitled to join and serve in the new National Army. They were Irishmen and, with their military skills, were essential as instructors, and combatants if necessary, in this new beginning. It would be totally untrue to charge that recruits were accepted *from* the British forces. In any case, those who did join the National Army after previous military service elsewhere were a very small percentage of the new recruitment. It should be pointed out that ex-British soldiers had been accepted into the IRA before, as well as after the Truce. Tom Barry was one such soldier. Emmet Dalton, W.R.E. Murphy, Dermot MacManus and A.T. (Tony) Lawlor had distinguished service in the British Army prior to joining the pre-Truce IRA. In the advance into Tralee in the Civil War, a companion soldier was killed beside the author by gunfire from defence points manned by anti-Treaty troops whose unit included three ex-British soldiers. Another ex-British service man, Con Healy, a crack marksman, serving with A Company 1st (Tralee) Battalion IRA, was chosen to shoot Major McKinnon, a notorious Auxiliary company commander, on the old Tralee golf course that straddled Racecourse Road, in March 1921. A British soldier named Reginald Hathaway, serving with his regiment in Tralee, deserted to the IRA and took the anti-Treaty side in the Civil War. With two comrade soldiers, he was captured in arms and all three were executed by Free State firing-squad in Ballymullen barracks, Tralee, on 25 April 1923.

Clearly, the acceptance of men who had learned their military skills in the British service was not without precedent in 1922. The Civil War brought in the most colourful of them on the anti-Treaty side in the person of swashbuckling 'Deadeye Dave' (Captain David Robinson), who had been a commander 'in tanks' in the 1914-18 war in which he had lost an eye; an old friend of Erskine Childers, his Irish war service was mainly in Kerry. Another extraordinary character was Billy Whelan who came from the United States to fight on the anti-Treaty side. He had been a property salesman in Florida. Standing no more than five feet two in his stockinged feet, he remained in Kerry after the Civil War ended and helped Sinn Féin Dáil candidates with their election campaigns.[71]

On 20 July, the Provisional Government announced that its forces were in supreme control in Leinster, and in Monaghan, Cavan, Roscommon, Leitrim and Clare. Some resistance was being encountered in Donegal and Sligo, with some hard opposition in Galway, Limerick and Tipperary; Waterford, Cork, Kerry and Mayo were 'in subjection' to the anti-Treaty forces.

On 21 July, the Provisional Government was able to report that Waterford had been captured by National Army troops on the 20th; and on the following day that Limerick and Sligo had also fallen to them. Subsequently, troops under Sean MacEoin and his second in command, Colonel A.T. Lawlor, moved from Athlone to take control of towns along the Roscommon, Sligo and Mayo border areas, to link eventually with Government forces that had landed from the sea at Westport and with other units that had won control in Galway city.

Thus, the Provisional Government had effectively established its authority in major areas of the country within a month of the Four Courts attack. Establishing authority, however, did not mean the end of combat in those areas; the war would continue for ten months to come, largely in the form of guerilla action by anti-Treaty flying columns which inflicted heavy casualties in dead and wounded and caused enormous damage to the countryside. The significance of the position, however, was that there was no longer the possibility of a revolutionary overthrow of the Provisional Government. Furthermore, the sorting out of military loyalties and the wholehearted welcome being given to the National Army by the population in general enabled those in power to plan with confidence for the future of both civil and military affairs.

Nevertheless, despite the gains and the confidence, the immediate future looked grimly forbidding. As uncertainty about the future of their cause grew, the anti-Treatyites burned barracks and coastguard stations in areas they were evacuating, as well as burning other buildings that might also be of use to the National Army. They trenched roads, thus preventing the holding of fairs and markets, interfering with industry and commerce, and even with the supply of food to some towns. Such actions, aimed at preventing the Provisional Government from governing, eventually became part of their strategy. 'We have to build with one hand and fight with the other,' exclaimed Kevin O'Higgins.

By the end of the third week in July, the anti-Treaty forces in the south, driven from Waterford and the key city of Limerick, were pressed into a general defence area extending roughly from Dungarvan in County Waterford, via Carrick-on-Suir, Callan, Clonmel, Kilmallock and Newcastlewest, to Listowel in County Kerry. It was what remained of the so-called defence line by which Liam Lynch had planned to seal off the greater portion of Munster from the rest of the country. He believed he could hold it long enough to force the Provisional Government to negotiate a settlement, and any settlement that would acknowledge the Free State was far from his mind. In fact, 'the line' had no existence in a military sense. In the words of one writer, it 'had little more substance than the Equator'.[72] All it amounted to was a number of strongly held but unco-ordinated and widely separated defence positions extending across the province from Limerick in the west, following main roads and the River Suir, to Waterford in the east. All the territory south of these positions, which comprised a great part of the counties of Limerick, Tipperary and Waterford and the whole of Cork and Kerry, was controlled by the anti-Treatyites and they were pledged to defend it to the last.

The loss of Limerick and Waterford meant that the defence line, such as it was, had been cut at both ends. Attacks against the centre positions were then launched by troops from the 1st and 2nd Eastern Divisions and from Tipperary, Kilkenny and Waterford, aided by detachments of the Dublin Guards. Numerically, the anti-Treatyites outnumbered them but they were outwitted and also outmatched in the matter of resources and unit control. They fought largely as separate units, with dedication as befitted their commitments, but they were without cohesion or any kind of operational plan because of the earlier indecision and lack of preparedness by their leaders.

In Dublin, Oscar Traynor was arrested while attempting to pass through a National Army patrol at Baggot Street Bridge on 27 July. This could be considered a serious blow to the anti-Treaty cause in the city, where the remnant of his Dublin Brigade had maintained a sporadic warfare since the Four Courts and Sackville Street fighting. Despite Traynor's arrest, however, attacks continued, with special emphasis on sniper fire on patrols and barracks. His brigade had suffered greatly in the matter of casualties and arrests, and due to disintegration was unable to attempt a combined operation against the Provisional Government in the College of Science building in Merrion Street, or against the National Army GHQ now in Portobello barracks. Its inadequacy was heightened by the fact that so many of the active service fighting men of the pre-Truce Dublin Brigade had thrown in their lot on the side of the Free State, and were generally aware of the identity and resources of their adversaries.

There was fighting in Dundalk where fortunes swayed, and in parts of Wexford, Kilkenny, Donegal, Mayo and Sligo, but the real confrontation lay southwards. In fact, Richard Mulcahy believed that the 'only definite military problem' confronting the National Army was in the south.[73]

The cost of a frontal offensive against the Liam Lynch defences across Munster and of subsequently fighting every inch of the way against a formidable foe, through difficult campaigning country, rendered more so by extensive destruction of roads, railway lines and bridges, was a daunting prospect for the National Army Command to contemplate. Such was the situation on 15 July when Richard Mulcahy in Portobello barracks sent Michael Collins 'a list of vessels which can be made available as troop transports'.[74] Provision of the list in mid-July suggests that Emmet Dalton's proposal for sea-borne troops to be landed in the rear of anti-Treaty strongholds in the south was under consideration by GHQ, if not already accepted, at least a week prior to the fall of Limerick and Waterford.

Plans to put Dalton's advice to test were immediately set in train. An expeditionary force would be sent by sea from Dublin to Westport, County Mayo. The vessel chosen, the *Arvonia,* was fitted out in Dublin. Carrying some 400 troops under Colonel-Commandant Christopher (Kit) O'Malley of the Dublin Guards, she steamed around the northern coast and down to Clew Bay. Her deck cargo included an armoured car and an eighteen-pounder field piece.

The expedition arrived in Clew Bay at dawn on Monday, 24 July. Because the *Arvonia* was a hundred feet too long for Westport pier, disembarkation was delayed, but a detachment of forty troops was put ashore in boats commandeered from fishing vessels in the bay. Without a shot being fired, these troops surprised and captured an anti-Treaty party of twelve in a nearby coastguard station. The main body of O'Malley's force landed later and went on to take Westport without encountering resistance and link up with units of Sean MacEoin's Western Command in Castlebar and Sligo for further operations.

Despite the success of the Clew Bay expedition, a note of caution about an early landing on the Cork and Kerry coast was struck by two important generals, one of whom was immediately concerned with the National Army offensive in the south-west Munster sector; this was Eoin O'Duffy, OC South Western Command. It was his opinion that any such landing 'at the present time' must meet with disaster.[75] On 25 July, at an hour when it was thought at GHQ in Dublin that a landing from the *Arvonia* could not be effected at Westport, a dispatch was sent by Richard Mulcahy to inform O'Duffy in Limerick that he had 'this morning wired Comdt. O'Malley, who is in charge of the expedition, to go to Limerick and report to you. You may disembark the troops at Limerick as you think fit, or you may consider the question of a landing at Tralee, but if you face the latter question you will want carefully to consider the place of landing there, as the boat was 100 feet too long to land at Westport.'[76]

O'Duffy's response left no room for doubt about his dislike of the idea of a landing at Tralee (meaning Fenit) at that time: 'I would consider a landing at Tralee, or anywhere on the Cork or Kerry coast, unwise for the present,' he advised Mulcahy next day, 26 July. 'There would be an immediate concentration of Irregulars,' he believed, 'and our troops would be immediately surrounded. They might make a fight but I fear that would be all. While landing in a friendly territory is very advantageous, still if the local [pro-Treaty] Volunteers are not organized they are of very little military value.'[77]

Six days later, an expeditionary force of some 450 Dublin Guards under the command of Brigadier Paddy O'Daly left Dublin on board the *Lady Wicklow*. They were Fenit bound.

It seems clear now that Michael Collins, as Commander-in-Chief of the National Army, had, with his accustomed speed, already taken over the active direction of military operations, particularly the sea-borne landings. Significant of his involvement in the planning was the selection of officers to lead the landings. They were chosen from men who were close to him in Dublin and upon whose loyalty, fighting qualities and experience he depended: Christopher O'Malley for Westport, Paddy O'Daly for Fenit, and Emmet Dalton and Tom Ennis for Cork. There is reason to believe that the decision to send the expedition to Fenit was a hurried one, taken by the Commander-in-Chief after failure to co-ordinate plans with Treaty supporters in Tralee. It is frustrating that widespread search has failed to locate an operational order or military directive relative to the task force.

Paddy O'Daly's Dublin Guards effected a surprise landing from the *Lady Wicklow* at the port of Fenit on Wednesday 2 August 1922, and captured Fenit and Tralee on the same day. The anti-Treatyites, who belonged to the 8th Battalion, Kerry No 1 Brigade, burned the coastguard station, which had been their garrison post, and then retired. In unpublished notes,[78] John Martin O'Connor, the Ballylongford Company Captain, has recorded that his active service unit burned the former RIC barracks at Ballylongford and Ballybunion early on the same morning, after which actions all the 8th Battalion active service units withdrew to Duagh and Knocknagoshel via Ballyloughran.

Next day, a detachment of 240 tough troops of the 1st Western Division under Colonel-Commandant Michael Hogan landed at Tarbert in north Kerry without opposition. They had simply crossed the Shannon from Kilrush in three small vessels. Hogan put a garrison of twenty-five men into the former RIC barracks in Tarbert, which was in a rather ruinous condition, and then pushed rapidly ahead. By early evening he had occupied Ballylongford (where he took six prisoners) and reoccupied Listowel, both towns falling to him without opposition. He set up a garrison post in O'Rahilly's house in Ballylongford. The Listowel anti-Treaty garrison withdrew towards Abbeyfeale, having first burned the courthouse, the workhouse and the former RIC barracks.

Hogan's force contained a small number of men who had left Tralee because of their refusal to accept the dictates of local anti-Treaty leaders. Included in the group were William J.(Billy) Clifford, Jack Flavin, Stephen Scannell, Jimmy Lyons, Tom Slattery and Harold Reid. In Listowel they were named 'The Dandy Six'.[79] They were now free to join Eamon Horan, the senior pro-Treaty IRA member in Tralee, in forming a separate Kerry force to strengthen O'Daly, whose next mission was to advance across the county via Castleisland, Farranfore, Killarney and Rathmore, and eventually link with Cork troops at Millstreet and with troops of General W.R.E. Murphy's command at Newcastlewest.

On 8 August, troops from Dublin under Emmet Dalton and Tom Ennis effected landings at Passage West, Union Hall and Youghal in County Cork. The anti-Treatyites, caught off guard again, lost Cork city within a few days. On 10 August, Kerry No 2 Brigade National Army troops under Brigadier Tom 'Scarteen' O'Connor, accompanied by 1st Northern troops from their training-centre at the Curragh, sailed from Limerick round the Kerry coast and, on the following day, occupied Kenmare without opposition. O'Connor subsequently captured Cahirciveen and Waterville and thus held three coastal towns in the Kerry IRA No 2 and No 3 Brigade areas.

The sea-borne landings in the south, introduced as an encirclement manoeuvre by the War Council of the Provisional Government in August 1922, caused the early collapse of the remaining defence positions in the anti-Treaty 'front' in Munster. The Kerry landing was the most problematic. In Westport the landings had the co-operation of local pro-Treatyites. The Passage West expedition was accompanied by Cork pro-Treaty officers. Before Kenmare there was a secret visit to Dublin by the 'Scarteen' brothers, Tom and John O'Connor.

In Tralee, the situation was different. The town and district were in the area of Kerry No 1 Brigade IRA, and the two Tralee battalions, the 1st and a newly formed 9th, were overwhelmingly anti-Treaty. Collins's link with Eamon Horan was tenuous at best and probably non-existent. Difficulties of the kind were surmountable in the minds of Collins and O'Daly. Even though there was nobody on board the *Lady Wicklow* with knowledge of Fenit or Tralee as far as O'Daly knew, this did not deter him. He could not have known that the most experienced fighting men under arms from the three Kerry brigades were for the major part helping to hold Lynch's defence positions in the counties of Limerick, Tipperary and Waterford, or otherwise were prisoners of the National Army; or that a secret action carried out by non-combatants at dead of night had greatly reduced the effectiveness of the anti-Treaty garrison at Fenit.

It was only at this time that an army communications system was given urgent planning attention. Wireless telegraphy sets were purchased and distributed to operational areas, and radio personnel with merchant shipping experience were enlisted to commissioned ranks in order to promote the training of army signal personnel. The overall responsibility for the development of communications devolved on Major Liam Archer, a 1916 man who had worked closely with Collins's intelligence service during the Anglo-Irish War. He later became Chief of Staff of the Irish Army with the rank of Lieut-General.

Eamon Horan joined Paddy O'Daly's troops in Tralee and,

with the rank of commandant, began the formation of the separate Kerry unit of the National Army immediately after the capture of the town. He had the following advertisement published in *The Kerry People*.[80]

AN APPEAL TO THE MEN OF KERRY

Men are required immediately to fill
the ranks of the Official Republican Army.
Recruits will be inspected for acceptance on
their presenting themselves at Ballymullen Barracks.
We will lead you to complete independence,
as we led you to where you are now.
Signed: Comdt. Eamon Horan,
Official Republican Army.
Ballymullen Military Barracks,
Tralee 4.8.'22.

Readers not acquainted with the intricacies of thought that marked the Treaty age will wonder at the description 'Official Republican Army'. They may accept the declaration by so many pre-Truce IRA men who were on one side or the other in the Civil War that those of their comrades of the War of Independence who were for the Treaty were as much republican in mind as those who were against it; they differed only in the approach. The Provisional Government claimed the pro-Treaty army to be the 'National Army' or the 'Regular Irish Republican Army', and referred to the anti-Treaty army as the 'Irregulars' or the 'Mutineers'. The pro-Treaty army became known to everybody as the Free State Army or just the 'Staters', months before the Free State was legally established on 6 December 1922. Likewise, the anti-Treaty army became the Republican Army, although the leaders of the anti-Treaty side of the Sinn Féin party in Dáil Éireann from de Valera down (as well as the leaders of the pro-Treaty side) had, months before the Treaty was signed, abandoned all hope of wresting a republic from the British at that time. All realized that they must settle for less.

Paradoxically, it took another war to bring the two sides

together. The world war of 1939-1945 saw the entry of great numbers of Civil War Republicans into the National Defence Forces, where they found common cause with one-time adversaries in protecting our neutral position. In that acceptance of common cause, one may quote what Michael Collins wrote in acceptance of the Treaty, shortly before his tragic death: 'If any power menaces our liberties, we are in a stronger position than before to repel the aggressor. The position will grow stronger with each year of freedom if we all unite for the aims we have in common.'[81]

The landing of the Dublin Guards at Fenit was the most spectacular and possibly the most effective of the August encirclement operations. What follows is a reconstruction of the landing and the fight for Tralee, which was taken from the anti-Treaty forces on the same day. I was a participant and I wrote an account of the operation simply as a record for the Military Archives Section of the Army at GHQ Dublin. Later, I thought of the account as a possible booklet and I expanded its scope on the suggestion of my friend Dan Nolan, to whom I am indebted for his valuable assistance, especially in obtaining the recollections of several surviving members of the forces that opposed us, the story of the brave anti-Treaty Cumann na mBan girls who tended our wounded, and the non-combatant eyewitness accounts of the actions at Fenit, Sammy's Rock and the Spa. Sadly, the survivors were few in number, but they included the commandants of the two Tralee battalions, John Joe Sheehy of the 1st and Paddy Paul Fitzgerald of the 9th. In the words of Con Casey, one time Adjutant Kerry No 1 Brigade IRA, the task was undertaken ten or more years too late.

This introduction, lengthy though it be, is essential to an appreciation of a Free State officer's view of the military [IRA] situation after the approval of the Anglo-Irish Treaty by Dáil Éireann on 7 January 1922. Throughout what follows, the armies of the tragic divide are referred to as the Free State Army and the Republican Army.

Niall C. Harrington

1

FROM BOYLE TO BEGGARS' BUSH

An enforced change of course in my not uneventful young life led me to be a soldier of the Dublin Guards aboard the *Lady Wicklow* steaming towards Fenit on the sunny Wednesday morning of 2 August 1922.

I was born in Dublin in 1901, reared in Tralee where I attended the Christian Brothers' school in Edward Street and I obtained my secondary school education at Rockwell College in County Tipperary. My ambition was to be a pharmaceutical chemist, and on leaving Rockwell in June 1918 I was apprenticed to chemist James Barry in Boyle, a pleasant town beautifully situated in north County Roscommon. There my lot seemed happily cast following a career in the profession of my choice. But Boyle was a garrison town and the sight of khaki-clad British soldiers tramping the streets was hard on the eyes. Early in 1919 I joined the Irish Volunteers.

Inevitably, my joining of the Volunteers was influenced by family background as well as boyhood observation of the new Ireland that was rising from the ashes of Easter Week. My father, Tim Harrington, was a Nationalist MP at Westminster from 1880 to his death in March 1910. He was secretary of the National League, which replaced the suppressed Land League, and was the author of the Plan of Campaign. The basic idea of the Plan was to withhold excess rents and use the money for the protection of tenant farmers in case of eviction. In the bitter years of the land war, my father suffered many terms of imprisonment. He remained faithful to Parnell after the disastrous split in the Nationalist party. As Dublin's Lord Mayor, 1901-03, he declined an invitation to attend the ceremonies connected with the coronation of Edward VII in

London in 1903. Powerful pressure to attend was brought to bear on him by the influential forces of Dublin Unionism, especially as represented in the Corporation. It was well known in such circles that he had the offer of a choice of three tempting appointments as an inducement to accept the invitation. They were the recordership of Dublin, a county court judgeship or a colonial governorship. Unionists were aghast when he turned down the offer and later rejected the reward of a knighthood by declining to receive King Edward on the occasion of his official visit to Dublin in the same year.

After my father's death I was sent to Tralee to live with his brother Dan at Nelson (now Ashe) Street. That was in the autumn of 1910. My mother remained in Dublin and my sisters were sent to boarding-school at Mount Sackville convent. My uncle Dan printed and published *The Kerry Sentinel,* a provincial weekly newspaper which was founded by my father in 1877, shortly after he had gone from his native Castletown-bere, County Cork, to teach in Tralee at Holy Cross Seminary, a Dominican school for boys, at 1 Day Place. Long extinct, *The Sentinel* was a Land League paper in every sense.

Along with my school friends Jerry Myles and Patrick (Percy) Hanafin, I joined the Fianna on the early formation of a *sluagh* in Tralee. Both of these friends were of intensely patriotic families who suffered greatly for their part in the fight for freedom. Jerry was seriously wounded in the successful action against the RIC at Castlemaine in 1921. His brother Billy fell fighting on the Republican side in the Civil War. Percy Hanafin died of wounds received in a shoot-out with Truce-breaking Black and Tans at Edward Street, Tralee, in January 1922.

My membership of the Fianna was of no active importance, merely indicating a trend of thought that influenced decisions of later years.

In August 1914, at the outbreak of the first world war, I watched the long ranks of the Kerry Militia and the Munster Fusiliers march from Ballymullen barracks to entrain at Tralee railway station en route to their decimation on the battlefields of France and Belgium. 'Your King and country need you,' was the early recruiting slogan on posters featuring the British War Minister, Lord Kitchener, who first glimpsed the light of day from Gunsborough House near Listowel.

Other forces were marching and drilling with hurleys and wooden guns. The Irish Volunteer movement had reached Tralee and as a boy I watched the men assemble in Denny Street and often followed them on their marches. On Sunday, 27 February 1916, I followed them from their headquarters at the Rink at Basin View to the Sportsfield (now the Austin Stack Memorial Park), where they were received by Padraig Pearse. They were armed and, headed by the Tralee Volunteer pipers' band, were greeted enthusiastically as they marched through the town. I was present that night at the Rink for a concert and a lecture given by Pearse on 'The Nature of Freedom'. The concert was in aid of the Jack McGaley Indemnity Fund. The Rink was packed for the occasion. McGaley, a popular local man who had been dismissed by his employer because of his Volunteer activities, was serving a prison term with hard labour under the Defence of the Realm Act — better known as DORA.

The review and lecture cloaked the real reason for the presence of Pearse in Tralee so close to the Rising. He had come to give Austin Stack, Commandant of the Kerry Regiment of Volunteers and head of the IRB in the county, the confidential information that the Rising was to take place on Easter Monday, and that a shipload of arms from Germany was due at Fenit pier on Easter Sunday night. He wanted to confer with him and Father Joe Breen, Chaplin to the Kerry Volunteers, on the landing and distribution of the guns, and gave orders that the necessary preparations were to be made under strict maximum secrecy. Nothing was to happen, not a shot was to be fired, before the evening of Easter Sunday.

On Easter Sunday, the Kerry Volunteers assembled at the Rink to receive orders. But the arms-bearing *Aud* had already come and gone, on Holy Thursday. The late change in the arrival date of the shipment, whether made by the German Admiralty or by the secret Military Council of the IRB in Dublin, had not been communicated to Austin Stack.

The following day Roger Casement and two companions were put ashore from a German submarine. The Kerry Volunteer leadership had no knowledge of their coming, and neither had the Military Council; Casement was not part of any of their plans for the Rising. He had come to advise the leaders to postpone it, as he believed the armoury in the *Aud* was not sufficient. If they did not agree, he was prepared to join them in the fight. Casement was arrested by two members of the RIC who found him resting in an old fort near Ardfert on Good Friday. He was brought to the constabulary barracks in Tralee that evening, a brief stop off on the way to the inevitable gallows in London. His coming led to the arrest of Austin Stack, also on Good Friday — the one man who knew all the plans for Kerry. So, through no fault of theirs, the Kerry Volunteers took no part in the Rising.

James Feely, captain of Boyle Company of the Volunteers, had already acquired a name and reputation as a militant 'Sinn Féiner', following his arrest and imprisonment on conviction of leading a raid for arms at Rockingham House, home of the King Harman family, in February 1918, when rifles, shot-guns and ammunition were seized. Jim, as I learnt to call him, was a stalwart character and the fortunate possessor of a keen sense of humour that relieved many a difficult situation. Through him I was enrolled in the Volunteers.

Although Volunteer activity throughout the country in 1919 was largely devoted to organizing and the building of communications and intelligence, armed combat took place as well, notably in Munster. The western counties came late into the fight and were not as effectively active in the field in the winter of 1920 as from the spring of the following year, when the impact of reorganization and the formation of active service units resulted in many telling blows against the RIC and British military. Then the Roscommon men at Scramogue in March 1921, south Mayo men at Tourmakeady in May, and the west Mayo men at Carrowkennedy in May and June showed the enemy that the west was truly awake.

Boyle Company of the Volunteers had become A Company, 1st (Boyle) Battalion North Roscommon Brigade IRA. I became 1st lieutenant, by election, as was the custom of the time. Jim Feely was captain and his brother Henry 2nd lieutenant. It was through the Company Intelligence Officer, Paddy Doogue, an employee of the Midland Great Western Railway Company, that word was sent to Michael Collins conveying the information about Field Marshal Viscount French's movements and travel arrangements prior to the attack on him at Ashtown on 19 December 1919.

Lord French had been singled out for assassination because of what he represented in Ireland and not because of any animosity towards him personally. As British Viceroy, he was head of all the forces of repression in the country. He had a private residence at Frenchpark, some few miles outside Boyle and close to the Sligo–Roscommon border, to which he repaired from time to time. The most elaborate precautions were always taken for his safety and he never travelled anywhere without a strong military bodyguard. On this occasion, the information given to Collins was that Lord French, on his return from Frenchpark to the Viceregal Lodge in the Phoenix Park, would travel by train as far as Ashtown station on the north side of Dublin and thence by car for the short distance from there to the Lodge. The attack failed because Lord French, who was in mufti, switched from the second car, in which he usually travelled, to the first in the convoy of three, thereby saving his life. The second car was a total wreck by the roadside, its only occupant a wounded British soldier. The other two cars were driven off towards the Lodge at furious speed.

The attacking party, under the command of Paddy O'Daly of the GHQ Squad, sustained two casualties in the exchange of fire with the Viceroy's military guards. Martin Savage from Sligo, a lieutenant in the 2nd Battalion Dublin Brigade, was killed, and Dan Breen was wounded. Lord French escaped without a scratch. Many attempts were made to kill him. He had a charmed life.

We raided for arms in the districts around Boyle, Cootehall, Grange, Ballinameen and Kingsland. Although we raided by night it was difficult to avoid detection in a heavily garrisoned town such as Boyle, with police as well as military of the Bedfordshire Regiment patrolling during the curfew hours of night and early morning. Barry's place, where I worked and lived, was less than a hundred yards from the police and military barracks, and for me to return to base without being spotted when on my way back from some nocturnal escapade meant a close reconnaissance of the curfew patrols under cover of darkness. A quick dash at the right moment gained me the cover of a door in a laneway close to the shop. A pause to open the door, which was always left unlocked, then a climb on to the roof of an outbuilding allowed easy entrance through a back window of the house and I was home. Although this became a well-worn route it was never discovered. Nevertheless, it was not difficult for the police to find out who the active 'Shinners' were, and of course we became known to them. Barry's was raided from time to time and the house and everyone in it were thoroughly searched. Nothing was ever discovered although there was much to be found.

At Easter 1920, all unoccupied RIC barracks, together with income-tax records, in the 1st (Boyle) Battalion North Roscommon Brigade area were destroyed in response to a GHQ general order issued simultaneously to all units throughout the country. Our targets were Ballinameen, Knockvicar, Grevisk and Cootehall. My personal contribution to the destruction was the vacant Grevisk RIC station and the income-tax records and other documents at Cootehall, using petrol which had conveniently arrived at Boyle railway station for the use of the Bedfordshires. Mails were seized and there were other activities of a relatively minor kind, but, in the matter of combat participation in the mounting tempo of guerilla warfare, Boyle remained a quiet area. The boycott of goods of Belfast manufacture was enforced as part of our activities. We had our problems with Unionist business houses and, although we did not relish the task, we did whatever was necessary to ensure the total enforcement of the boycott in and around the town.

The social ostracism of the RIC decreed by our superiors gave rise to more serious problems. Members of the force were to be made social outcasts. Neither they nor their families were to be supplied with goods of any kind. This was disastrous for shopkeepers caught between our enforcement officers and the RIC. It was also disastrous for us. We put up notices to publicize the boycott, but we also had to call personally on shopkeepers to warn them against supplying the needs of the RIC, thus identifying ourselves positively as active members of the IRA. Whatever suspicion they might have attached to us previously was confirmed and those of us who were active in the enforcement of the boycott became marked men. Furthermore, the shopkeepers lost their merchandise. The RIC simply took what they wanted from the shops when they were not served, telling the shopkeepers to call to the barracks for payment. Needless to say, no shopkeeper would be seen calling to an RIC barracks at that time.

Among those who remained in the RIC after the wholesale resignations from the force in 1920 were some of our most bitter enemies. They included a number of officers and constables who were already involved in the British Government's new policy of murder and terror before ever the first of the Black and Tans had arrived in the country. On the other hand, a few of those who remained in the RIC risked their livelihood and even their lives by secretly working with the IRA.

A (Boyle) Company consisted of not more than twenty-five men in July 1920. It was kept small for security reasons. Pat Brennan became OC after Jim Feely was given command of the 1st (Boyle) Battalion. Martin Killilea became Quartermaster North Roscommon Brigade, and Pat Delahunty Brigade Intelligence Officer. There was an IRB circle in Boyle and I was sworn into the Brotherhood by Martin Killilea.

Early in August, four IRA officers in Boyle received notices referring to the boycott of the RIC, warning them to prepare for death. I was one of the four. The notices were signed 'All-Ireland Anti-Sinn Féin Society'. Having consulted among ourselves as to what we should do, we sent the notices to GHQ in Dublin with a request for instructions. The response we got simply told us to carry on with our normal work in daytime but sleep away at night, a very sensible directive, yet one not altogether easy to carry out. A bed was found for me in a schoolmaster's house out towards Doon, a couple of miles from the town. As it was summertime, the curfew patrol came late on duty and I had no problem so long as I kept to my sleeping-out arrangement. But one gets careless, and on 17 August I was working late and decided to stay the night rather than head towards Doon. The other occupants of the residential part of Barry's house were Phil Fahey, the shop manager, an elderly housekeeper and another apprentice, Frank Dooley, who shared a bedroom with me. Frank, an IRA man who had so far escaped suspicion, was arrested and interned later.

About two o'clock in the morning I was awakened by the manager opening the street door to an urgent voice asking for medicine. Next I heard the tread of many feet climbing the stairs. Not yet wide-awake, I hesitated too long about getting out through the back window. The bedroom door burst open and a number of masked men entered. A torch dazzled me. 'This is the man we're looking for,' a voice said. I was ordered out of bed and told to 'get down the stairs in front of us'. I attempted to pull on my trousers but was pushed ahead without them. 'You won't need clothes when we're finished with you,' said the same voice.

About half a dozen more masked men were in the hallway downstairs. I was punched and knocked down by a couple of them, and kicked about the floor. 'Take him out and let him have what's coming to him,' a new voice cut in. This, I knew, meant only one thing, and I was determined that if they brought me outside I would run for life rather than be shot where I stood. The laneway was only a few yards away, and I felt that there might be a chance of escaping from them. I did not have to try. Another voice said, 'Ah, give him a chance, he's only a kid.' There was a moment of fearful silence, then a warning that I would be shot unless the boycott was ended within three days. 'We'll get you no matter where you go,' I was told. With that, the masked men left, and as they moved off I saw that they were wearing the long black overcoats of the RIC.

That same night Jim Feely was dragged from bed and on to the roadway. He made a bolt for freedom and shots were fired as he vaulted some railings. He got away and spent the remainder of the morning uncomfortably in a gully that opened on to the railway line close to where he lived. Pat Brennan was caught at home and beaten insensible. The masked men also sought Pat Delahunty, but he was not at home when they called. It was disquieting that the raids should have taken place on a night when three of the four of us who had received the threatening notices could be found at home by the RIC.

Years afterwards, Pat Delahunty told me in the course of a letter that, as Brigade IO, he got occasional information from District Inspector John Kearney of the RIC, who was then stationed in Boyle. Some time after the raids by the masked RIC men, he received a note from Kearney advising him to clear out of town and to tell Feely and Harrington to get out also. 'I met Kearney later,' he wrote, 'and he told me that Colonel Sharpe, who was in charge of the Auxiliaries [in Boyle], intended to shoot us as a reprisal for the boycott.' Kearney had entered Irish history some four years earlier when, as head constable in Tralee, he had custody of Roger Casement after his arrest at Banna strand on Good Friday 1916. He claimed after the Truce that he would have facilitated the rescue of Casement by the Kerry Volunteers if an attempt had been made. Be that as it may, it is beyond question that he was in contact with IRA Intelligence during the 1920-21 period.

Kearney had an eventful few weeks as a Deputy Commissioner of the Civic Guard in the spring of 1922 before the hostility of IRA recruits in the new police force resulted in his resignation and probably caused his abrupt departure for England. He had been recognized by recruits from Kerry and they accused him of betraying the beardless Casement by identifying him in Tralee RIC barracks. During the voyage from Wilhelmshaven to Tralee Bay on board the German submarine U19, Casement had shaved off his give-away of a beard by way of disguise.

It was evident that the RIC had a great deal of information about us and our movements. There was no question of withdrawing the boycott and little prospect of enforcing it either. In fact, our immediate concern was how to avoid arrest, if not a bullet. Jim Feely went on the run. He was well placed to do so for he had the support of his family and their many relations and connections. In a sense, I was but a bird of passage in Boyle and could not count on such aids to freedom and a ripe old age. The reality of my position had already been brought home to me when I urged action against the curfew patrol. 'It's all right for you,' I was told. 'You have nothing to lose, but our homes would be burned and our families terrorized.' This was indeed true. It was also true that some of the worst of the terror was being perpetrated in areas that were not yet fully into the guerilla war with the British.

My employer was not happy with the situation in his shop, and with good reason. I remained at work but had become an object of curiosity to the cash customers and a sort of magnetic attraction that drew members of the RIC to the shop. They took what they wanted without parting with any money. The untenable situation ended towards the end of September 1920, when Brigade QM Martin Killilea informed me that I was to take a dispatch to the Quartermaster-General, Michael Staines, in Dublin. I was given the dispatch and a sum of money for arms, and then went with Martin to Carrick-on-Shannon, where I took the train to Dublin. The RIC were keeping a close watch on all railway stations. They could have identified me at Boyle and probably telephoned ahead to Dublin. For that reason my ticket was bought for departure from Carrick, ten miles away.

I said good-bye to Martin. We went opposing ways in the Civil War. He spent long periods in internment during both the War of Independence and the Civil War and his health was greatly undermined. In later years we met frequently. He never married and lived alone in a large farmhouse at the Rock of Doon, looking out across the beautiful Lough Key. Happy in each other's company and with a bottle and two glasses on the table, we reminisced about old times and the great hopes and dreams of our early days. He was deeply bitter about the circumstances of his capture by British forces early in 1921. He believed he had been betrayed by the father of a comrade who was captured with him. It was a sad thought and it remained with him until his death in the late sixties.

Martin Killilea was the strong man in the north Roscommon area. He possessed courage, reliability and the quality of leadership. Were it not for his capture, he would undoubtedly have been OC of the North Roscommon Brigade as reorganized by Sean Connolly of Ballinalee in the winter of 1920-21 on the orders of Michael Collins and Richard Mulcahy.

The Quartermaster-General, Michael Staines, operated from an office under cover of the recently established New Ireland Assurance Company. It was located at the corner of Bachelor's Walk and Sackville Street, over Kapp and Peterson's tobacco shop. I called there and gave him the dispatch and money from the North Roscommon Brigade.

In Dublin I stayed first with my cousin Tim Harrington and his family at 15 Richmond Road. He was one of the Tralee Harringtons, a son of my uncle Dan. An unsuccessful search for work followed my business with the Quartermaster-General. My wish was to return to Boyle but it did not appear to be practical. I sought out Michael Knightly, formerly of Ballyard, Tralee, and then a journalist on the staff of the *Irish Independent*. I knew him and knew he would give me sound advice. He had fought in Dublin in the Rising and was close to the men at the head of the independence movement. On the establishment of the Irish Free State he was appointed editor of Dáil Debates and was Chief Press Censor during the war years 1939-1946.

Michael Knightly brought me to a secret meeting where I was called upon to give an account of the IRA situation in the area from which I had been expelled. He did not tell me beforehand who I would meet, but in the backroom in Lalor's Ecclesiastical Candle Manufacturing Company at Ormond Quay, Dublin, I met the Minister for Defence, Cathal Brugha, and the Minister for Home Affairs, Austin Stack. I was treated with courtesy and great consideration by these two leaders. They refused my request to be returned to north Roscommon as an IRA organizer. At nineteen I was too young, they said, and in any case I should have attended a training course to fit me for such work. The class was then concluding.

At the end of the interview Cathal Brugha asked me what I proposed doing with myself. Did I have any work or prospects? When I told him I had neither, he at once offered me employment in his factory. I recall his words clearly. 'I have no vacancy,' he said, 'but I will give you a job at thirty shillings per week.' I greatly appreciated his offer. In those days thirty shillings a week (£1.50) was sufficient to live on. As a pharmacy apprentice in Boyle I received no wage, only my board and lodgings. I thanked Cathal Brugha and told him that I would continue to try for employment with a chemist and so continue my studies. I never did succeed, despite help from Cathal Brugha and Michael Knightly and the fact that Austin Stack gave me his personal introduction to two Dublin city chemists, both staunch supporters of the independence movement.

Shortly after my interview with Cathal Brugha, I was walking one day near Findlater's Church at Parnell Square when I met Charlie Dalaigh, a member of the patriotic family of that name from Knockane, Firies, about eight miles south-east of Tralee. We had been at the Tralee Christian Brothers' school in Edward Street together before I went to Rockwell, but he was a few years ahead of me. Our conversation turned to our immediate circumstances, and when I mentioned my attempt to get a posting as an IRA organizer he told me that he had recently completed the training course and had just been appointed by Cathal Brugha to organize the IRA in Tyrone. He was to become OC 2nd Northern Division in May 1921. His commission, confirmed by Cathal Brugha in November of the same year, is now the only document of its kind in existence and is in the National Museum.

Tragically, on 14 March 1923, Charlie Dalaigh and three comrades of the Republican 2nd Northern Division (the Drumboe Martyrs) died in Drumboe Castle, Stranolar, County Donegal, facing a firing-squad of their countrymen. It was a reprisal execution, one of the shameful deeds that marked the course of the unhappy conflict of brother against brother.

I moved about from place to place in Dublin and worked at odd unhappy jobs, never for more than thirty shillings a week. One day a young man named Paddy Howard called on me at Richmond Road with a dispatch from Michael Collins. It was briefly worded and to the effect that I should not return to Boyle, where I would either be shot or beaten up by the police. The dispatch was initialled 'M.O'C'. I kept it in an otherwise empty match-box in my pocket for some time.

Eventually I burned it; it was too dangerous to keep, but I have regretted doing so ever since. I should have held it, not only as a proud memento of those times, but more as an indication of the extraordinary character of Michael Collins who, despite the immensity of his work and responsibilities, could give thought to the safety of one lone and unimportant Volunteer.

By this time I had received my transfer from A Company, 1st (Boyle) Battalion North Roscommon Brigade, to C Company, 2nd Battalion Dublin Brigade. My company captain was Tom Burke. We paraded as and where required, but always on Thursday evenings in the fields at the back of the new Marino schools in Fairview. Out of my weekly wage of thirty shillings I paid a weekly contribution of sixpence to company funds, collected by QM Jimmy Brennan at each Thursday parade. Jimmy was to lose an arm when fighting with the Republican forces in the Civil War. My immediate superior was the Company Intelligence Officer, Colman O'Donovan, who later served in the Diplomatic Service of the Free State.

We had a training and assembly house in North Great George's Street and there, in May 1921, with five members of my company, I had the privilege of attending the first classes of instruction in the new submachine-gun called the Thompson gun. We sat in a semi-circle facing the instructor, a former US Army captain named Patrick Cronin, who had fought in France during the first world war. He simply talked to us about the gun, its fire capacity, mechanism, range and combat usefulness. We did not fire it, but merely handled it in the course of the instruction. Cronin and another ex-US Army officer, Major James Dinneen, who had been a battalion commander in France from 1917 to the end of the war, had smuggled two Thompsons into Ireland for demonstration to the IRA. Both Cronin and Dinneen were Irish born. The guns were brought in on the initiative of Michael Collins and demonstrated in the house in North Great George's Street. One was fired in an attack on a troop train taking newly arrived British reinforcements from Amiens Street railway station to Kingsbridge en route to the Curragh. It was the first Thompson fired in battle. The attack took place in the morning of 16

June at a point on the railway line midway between Drumcondra Road and Botanic Road.

The gun was formally demonstrated in the presence of Collins, Mulcahy, Gearoid O'Sullivan, Tom Barry and six members of the Squad. The demonstration (one of a number) was satisfactory and 495 Thompsons, spare parts and magazines, and a large quantity of .45 calibre ammunition were brought in from the United States by Irish agents under the direction of Joe McGarrity. The entire lot was seized by customs officers and Department of Justice agents during a raid on the coal boat *East Side* on 16 June 1921, some twelve hours before she was due to sail from Hoboken, New Jersey. By coincidence, this happened on the day that the echo of the first Thompson gun fired in battle was heard in Dublin.

Forty-nine Thompsons of another lot did reach the IRA early in the Truce. Tom Barrett (Captain Tommy) of A Company 1st (Tralee) Battalion is shown holding one of the guns in the photograph of the take over of the staff barracks in Tralee from the British.

The *East Side* consignment of Thompsons was released to Clan na Gael representatives in September 1925 and sent by McGarrity to the IRA in the mid-thirties. Tom Barry took delivery of it in Cork Harbour, where it was off-loaded by sympathetic dockers. Sean Russell, the IRA Quartermaster-General, took about half of the consignment to Dublin where it wound up in the hands of Free State troops who had captured it.

I was not mobilized for the destruction of the Custom House on 25 May 1921, but had known of the task and the date for some time beforehand. At noon on the day it happened, I stood on O'Connell Bridge and watched the vast columns of smoke reaching into the sky from the burning buildings. In large measure, the destruction of all the public records and documents housed there spelled the collapse of British Civil Administration in Ireland. But the price was high. Of one hundred and twenty IRA men who took part in the operation, six were killed, twelve wounded and seventy captured. The men were drawn mostly from the 2nd Battalion, in whose area the Custom House stood. They were aided by men from the Squad and the Active Service Unit. Despite the loss of men and weapons, the British were not allowed to believe that they had struck a crippling blow at brigade strength. Activities were intensified by bombings and ambushes on street patrols by all units.

The Truce came unexpectedly on 11 July. It seemed vague and uncertain, until the fact sank home that the fear of death or capture had ceased to be part of our daily existence. We felt elated and stuck out a military chest as we were ordered into training camps when work permitted. My company trained at Kilmore House in Coolock, near Dublin. In the summer evenings we marched and sang and countermarched with patriotic fervour and learnt the tactics of conflict. Strange faces came among us — the Truce Volunteers. Recruiting had been opened and throughout the country young men joined in ever-increasing numbers, to some extent reminiscent of what had happened at the time of the conscription threat in 1918. The newcomers were untried by conflict, but were ready and eager to prove themselves. It was not altogether their fault that they had come late. As a security precaution, recruitment had been carefully screened and not greatly encouraged during the war years. The pre-Truce IRA was a closely knit organization in every brigade area, with probably not more than 5,000 men on active service in the entire country. The wisdom of open recruiting during the Truce has been strongly criticized. Assuredly, the recruitment provided fodder for the Civil War. Without the many thousands of new combat troops there would scarcely have been enough pre-Truce active service men on both sides to provide forces for serious conflict.

January 1922 brought the exciting and tumultuous days of the commencement of British withdrawal from twenty-six of our counties. The first barracks to be evacuated was Beggars' Bush in Dublin. In the third week of the month, 200 Auxiliaries marched from their depot at the Bush to Westland Row railway station, where they took the boat train for Kingstown. Their departure was muted; no colours, no music until they arrived at the harbour, where a military band played 'God Save the

King' as they embarked for their own country.

The air was full of wishful speculation. There was joyful thought too, despite the bitter debate in the Dáil before the deputies approved the Treaty on 7 January, 1922. It was joy before disillusionment.

Then it was 1 February 1922. The newspapers had announced that the first contingent of the new Irish Army would take over Beggars' Bush barracks on that day. The route to be taken by what the newspapers called 'The Soldiers of the Irish Nation' in a march of triumph was from an assembly point in the Phoenix Park, along streets that would take them past City Hall, where the salute would be taken by Arthur Griffith and Michael Collins; then by Dame Street, College Green and on to Beggars' Bush barracks, where the Minister for Defence, General Richard Mulcahy and the Chief of Staff, General Eoin O'Duffy, were waiting to greet the new regular soldiers and present them with colours.

Truly it was an emotional moment in my life and I felt a great stirring of pride as I watched the 1st Company of the Dublin Guard under Captain Paddy O'Daly march by in green uniform, with bright leather cross straps and boots and leggings and all the accoutrements of their new military life.

The uniform gave me much food for thought. A few weeks later, a friend who had been in the Bush, as the barracks was called, told me that a medical unit had been established there and that a chemist was part of the new set-up. I thought at once of my lost career and wondered if by enrolling in the new army I could get an assignment to the medical unit, and, in particular, to the chemist, and so resume my pharmaceutical studies. It was a fanciful idea, but youth is fanciful and in that long-ago time youth was vastly more naive than it is today. I sought out a man whom I knew, a distant relative, Major-General Piaras Beaslai, journalist and soldier, editor of the IRA journal *An tOglach*, and close friend of Michael Collins. He had his new offices at the Gresham Hotel, which had been temporarily taken over by the liaison and press groups of the new army. I called there and was given a letter of introduction to Commandant-General Leo (Stetto) Aherne, who was in charge of the Army Medical Corps in the Bush. Thus I came to be enrolled in what was described as the 'Irish Republican Army Medical Corps'.

I was posted to work under a chemist named Barry, not of course the Barry to whom I had been indentured in Boyle. I was in out of the cold and happy in my new surroundings. Of 'Stetto' Aherne's career I have no details, but I heard rumours which seemed to indicate that he had a more tuneful relationship with a gun than a stethoscope. He later served in the Cork Command. His office in the Bush was in one of a group of houses on the far left-hand side of the first square. The chemist had set up his dispensing department alongside. Both were Cork men.

In that beginning of the Army Medical Services, the Red Cross unit consisted of a doctor named King who had a practice in Blackrock, County Dublin. He attended the Bush in uniform and held the rank of captain. Working under him were two nurses, Marrinan and Clancy, together with Sergeant-Major Ned Skelly and Quartermaster John Jordan, both of whom were later commissioned; and some twenty or twenty-five privates like myself.

A hospital unit was established in the Bush before the King George V (now St Bricin's) and the Curragh hospitals were taken over, and Marrinan and Clancy became the first army nurses. Although I was a member of the Medical Corps, I was not, strictly speaking, a Red Cross man. I took part in the drills, including stretcher drill, and first-aid instruction, but most of my time was spent in the chemist's department. I had no wish to become a regular Red Cross man. I admired the vocation, if one likes to call it that, and in later combat I saw Red Cross soldiers bravely attend to casualties under fire.

In the pre-Truce period there were instances of active service by medical doctors who were themselves IRA men, but such examples were rare. It was rarer still to find doctors accompanying active service troops in the Civil War. The only doctor I knew to participate with Free State troops was Lieutenant Brigid Lyons (later Lyons Thornton) who was stationed at the Model Schools, Marlboro Street, Dublin, during the Sackville Street fighting in July 1922. Apart from the fact that she was an extremely attractive young woman, she had a record of active Cumann na mBan service before the Truce. She it was who brought Collins's plan for escape to Sean MacEoin when he was a badly wounded prisoner in King George V Hospital and facing the death sentence. The planned escape was prevented by the merest accident.

The Bush was the centre point for all activity. There was a continuous stream of country detachments passing through after being fitted out and having undergone brief training for the purpose of taking over barracks and posts from the British. The new uniform was becoming more noticeable in the city and there was a general drive towards smartening up the soldiers' appearance. Church parades with military bands and the national colours became a weekly event. The Dublin Guard, centred at the barracks, built its numbers mostly from the officers and men of the pre-Truce Dublin brigades, strengthened later by recruits from various outside areas. From the very beginning the unit developed a strong *esprit-de-corps* because of its fighting background and the fact that it was the first uniformed element of the new Irish Army. It owed its title to a small guard group formed by Mick McDonnell and Paddy O'Daly of the Dublin Brigade in 1919, at the request of Michael Collins. The group, which became better known as 'the Squad', operated directly under Collins; it was amalgamated with the Dublin Active Service Unit as a result of the losses sustained by both in the Custom House engagement in May 1921, and under the command of O'Daly the combined force was called the Dublin Guard.

In March the Dublin Guard became a battalion, a brigade in May, and O'Daly was promoted to the rank of brigadier. Later he became GOC Kerry Command. In the Civil War the Dublin Guard was referred to in the plural sense as 'the Dublin Guards'. The Dublin Brigade ceased to exist by that title with the foundation of regular battalions and brigades about February 1923.

From my vantage point in the pharmacy and because of the freedom I enjoyed in my capacity as assistant to the chemist,

I could observe the comings and goings to and from the Bush. Collins, of course, was a frequent visitor, accompanied by Dave Neligan, his close friend and guard; also several members of the GHQ Staff, the majority of whom had accepted the Treaty. All these people soon moved to Portobello barracks, which was taken over by Eastern Division troops under Commandant-General Tom Ennis, the notable OC of the 2nd Battalion Dublin Brigade in the War of Independence. In the early days I saw Sean Lemass and Mattie McDonnell enter the barracks in uniform. Both were lieutenants of my own company. They withdrew and fought on the Republican side in the Civil War. Amongst the outstanding Dublin personalities who were pro-Treaty, I saw Joe Leonard who had accompanied Emmet Dalton when, dressed in British Army uniform, they took a lead part in the attempt to rescue Sean MacEoin from Mountjoy prison; also Tom Keogh who shot the sentry on that occasion and secured the escape of the would-be rescuers, alas without MacEoin. Keogh was a particularly daring soldier. With Tom Cullen and Liam Tobin of the Intelligence Department, he was closest of all to Collins in Dublin, In September 1922, he and eight comrades were blown to pieces by a Republican trap mine at a bridge near Macroom, County Cork.

Other pro-Treaty officers I saw in the Bush were Jim McGuinness of the ASU, a strikingly brave and resourceful leader; and Jim Dempsey, also of the ASU, who was wounded in 1916. Another was Billy McClean who had a finger shot off in a fight in Mount Street with Auxiliaries from Beggars' Bush on Bloody Sunday. I saw the famous Frank Bolster of the Squad there, and met him again in Bantry, County Cork, during the Civil War. Two others who come to mind are Sean Guilfoyle and his brother Joe, both of whom had served under Commandant de Valera in 1916. Sean, a lieutenant in A Company, 3rd Battalion, was ordered by de Valera to lay siege to Beggars' Bush barracks, a tall order to an officer who had not more than seven or eight men with him.

Things were changing outside. A divided Irish Republican Army was emerging from the conventions and discussions were taking place in Dublin and throughout the country. There were those who declared for a republic, whole and entire, and opposed the 'stepping-stone' of Collins. Armed men were appearing everywhere. There was a vast confusion of ideologies, but little care for the wants of the people, 130,000 of whom were unemployed. The seizure of towns and buildings and the destruction of railway lines and bridges were putting an end to commerce in many places. The shootings, robberies and murders that were everyday occurrences were pauperizing the country and proof that law and order had ceased to exist.

Joy was giving way to disbelief on the part of the people. Inside Beggars' Bush there was much excitement and speculation as to whether the barracks might be seized from within by forces opposed to the Treaty. I recall the occasion when Eoin O'Duffy addressed a mass parade of troops in the barracks. He called on all present to declare their loyalty to the Provisional Government or declare themselves in conscience unable to do so. Those who were opposed were asked to take a pace forward. Surprisingly few did so. Only seven of the original company that entered the Bush on 1 February withdrew to fight on the Republican side in the Civil War.

In the first months of the year recruits were entering the Dublin barracks in a steady stream to join the new army. It was estimated at the time that by the beginning of May some 3,500 enlistments had taken place. There were various appellations to describe each side of the divided IRA. We were called Free Staters, which was quite true despite the nature of our enlistment into the Regular Irish Republican Army. We were, *de facto*, the National Army, acting under the authority of the Provisional Government. Idealistically, we considered ourselves republicans. Our opponents called themselves 'the Republicans', though to GHQ and the Government they were the 'irregulars'; they were also called diehards. At that time, ideology was largely a matter of where you happened to be at a particular moment of decision in your life.

In Dublin, after public buildings were seized by Republican forces as outposts for the Four Courts, which they occupied on 14 April 1922, there was firing everywhere. Sentries were patently nervous at their posts. Inside and outside Beggars' Bush barracks there was continuous firing at night.

At midnight on 27 June, I moved out of Beggars' Bush with a section of Red Cross men accompanying infantry troops on their way to surround the Four Courts. At 04.07 hours I heard the boom of the first shell directed at the Courts from a field-gun positioned at the corner of Winetavern Street and the quays. I remained in the vicinity of that gun when the crew moved it to Bridge Street and moved it back again to its original position. It was this changing of position which led to the belief that two field-guns shelled the Courts from the south side of the Liffey. A second gun, placed at St Mary's Abbey, was not brought into operational attack. The only field-gun used was operated by an inexperienced Free State gun crew. There was no British presence of any kind.

Shortly before the surrender on 30 June, I saw the enormous explosion which destroyed the public records of centuries. I crossed the bridge at Winetavern Street to see the surrender and watched Ernie O'Malley assembling the ranks of the garrison. 'Into line,' he called, 'and remember you are still soldiers of the republic.' I sought out former comrades and offered the token of cigarettes, but they turned away from me and disdained a handshake. Even Joe Griffin, whom I had known in boyhood in Tralee and subsequently in Dublin as an intelligence officer in the pre-Truce IRA and as a partner in the accountancy firm of MacDonagh and Boland, refused the acknowledgement of friendship. I entered the burning building at the Chancery Street side. The destruction was wholesale and terrible. Small arms and equipment of every kind, so scarce in the war with the British, littered the floors and passages. I stood to watch the flames eating into the great library.

After the initial madness I was back again in Beggars' Bush barracks. Soon afterwards I was stationed at Amiens Street railway station, and later at the Model Schools, Marlboro Street, during the Sackville Street fighting.

A great outbreak of activity followed the announcement of the 'National Call to Arms' by the Government on 7 July. The scheme was described as the 'Volunteer Reserve', and all men who joined since 28 June 1922 were classified as coming under it. The terms of service were six months or such shorter period as the Army Council might determine, and the rate of pay was three shillings and sixpence (17½p) per day and maintenance. Dependants' allowances were: Wife, four shillings (20p) per day; wife and child, five shillings and sixpence (27½p) per day; wife and two children, six shillings and sixpence (32½p) per day, and wife and three children, seven shillings and three pence (36¼p) per day. Permutations after the third child were not disclosed. The 'Call to Arms' brought into existence a national army of approximately 3,500 officers and 55,000 other ranks. By 1927, it had been reduced to 11,752 all ranks.

July 1922 was the month of decision for the Provisional Government. The warfare which had spread throughout the country was causing havoc to plans to build the new state. The situation had to be tackled and brought to a conclusion by the use of every source available to authority.

I had been growing away from the wish for a career in pharmacy, although I had been promoted to the 'rank' of corporal in the Medical Corps and felt properly proud of the blue insignia of rank around the sleeve of my tunic. Yet, though I was in the Medical Corps, I really was not of it, and some of my recent actions with infantry troops were not in any way related to what might be expected of a member of the medical unit. For one thing, I had been using a rifle from the roof of the Model Schools. Besides, I had consistently failed to put a Red Cross insignia on my tunic, another indication that I had not fully come to accept my medical posting.

On the night of 31 July, I marched from Beggars' Bush barracks for the last time.

1 T. C. Harrington, Nationalist MP at Westminster from 1880 to 1910, and Lord Mayor of Dublin from 1901 to 1903

Avondale - Rathdrum
Aug 18/84

My dear Harrington

I shall not be able to attend
meeting of Central Branch on Wednesday
as I am in the midst of my harvest
etc. Fenelon telegram just recd
from Strange; I have wired him
that I have written you asking you
to go down and consult with them; and
in your absence OBrien, or Healy
Please show the two latter this letter
A week since I wrote John OConnor of
Cork asking if he would stand, and
he has replied that he would prefer for several

2 *Letter from Charles Stewart Parnell to T. C. Harrington,
written from Avondale on 18 August 1884*

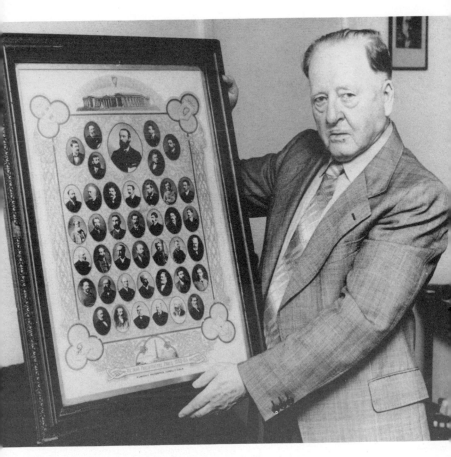

3 *Niall Harrington holds a photographic record of the Irish
Parliamentary Party 1880 to 1885*

4 *A Tralee Volunteer group in 1915. Front row: Danny Healy,*
Austin Stack, Alfred Cotton. Middle row: Michael Doyle,
Frank Roche, Danny Mullins, Eddie Barry. Back row:
Joe Melinn, Ned Lynch, Mick Fleming

5 *Members of the Squad: Mick McDonnell, Tom Kehoe, Vincent*
Byrne, Paddy O'Daly, Jim Slattery

6 Beggars' Bush barracks, Dublin

7 Beggars' Bush barracks, Dublin

8 *The Four Courts, shortly after noon on 30 June 1922, following the massive explosion which blew up the Records Office*

9 *Boyle barracks, Roscommon*

10 *Drawing for* An tOglach *by Sean Keating*

KEATING

*11 Liam Lynch, Chief of
Staff of the
Republican forces in
the Civil War*

12 Lady Wicklow, *the ship
that brought the Dublin
Guards to Fenit in
August 1922*

2

FENIT BOUND WITH THE
DUBLIN GUARDS

Towards the end of July 1922 the news broke that troops were about to be sent south by sea; to Cork, some of us thought, but nobody knew for certain. Whatever the destination, the news spelt adventure. Could I join the crowd going? I approached Lieutenant Jordan with the question, then Captain Skelly. No problem, and, truth to tell, I think they were relieved to be rid of an indeterminate and elusive member of their medical unit.

Not long afterwards I was on board the SS *Lady Wicklow* at her berth at the South Wall in Dublin. It was the night of Monday, 31 July 1922, and the time was 10.30. I had never been on any kind of ship before then. In my young life the sea had simply meant swimming at Fenit or Banna near Tralee, and to find myself on board a large seagoing passenger ship was something I had not given a thought to. It was a somewhat bewildering experience under the circumstances, the unfamiliar ship sounds and smells a background to the hustle and bustle of embarkation as hundreds of troops pounded the gang-planks with their nailed boots and sought a spot to lay their bodies, their weapons and kit-bags, a place to claim as their own for the duration of the voyage; or so they thought until the sea took over.

The armament we carried was formidable for that period of our military beginning. It consisted of one 18-pounder field piece, an armoured car named 'Ex-Mutineer' which had been captured at the Four Courts (where it had been 'Mutineer'); Lewis guns, rifles, ammunition in great quantities, grenades and grenade caps; tools of the trade for the task ahead. The armoured car was a Rolls-Royce 'Whippet', the type which the British had used most effectively against us. In fact, it was the first armoured car that they had handed over to the Provisional Government. Its armoured rotating turret housed a Vickers heavy calibre machine-gun, water cooled and capable of sustained firing without overheating. The car had changed sides a couple of times since it was handed over, in a period when it was not unusual for men to change sides.

The master of the *Lady Wicklow* was Captain John Theodore Rogers. Years afterwards I learned something about his ship. Built in the 1890s for the City of Dublin Steampacket Company, she had a length of 262 feet and a beam of thirty-four. Originally named *Wicklow*, along with her sister ships *Louth, Carlow* and *Kerry* she was taken over by the British and Irish Steampacket Company in 1919, and a year later all four were accorded the title *Lady*. Captain Rogers was not pleased when his *Lady* suddenly became an emergency troopship.

Despite the noise and the strange surroundings on board, I slept well on coils of rope. The bed was hard, but I was young. I was awakened by creaking woodwork and the throbbing sound of engines. It was the *Lady Wicklow* moving from her berth and heading towards the mouth of the Liffey, bound for a destination that was still unknown to all but a few of my fellow travellers and me, some 450 officers and men of the Dublin Guards. The time was five o'clock in the morning. I was told that late problems had delayed our departure, not least the failure of eighty troops from Wellington barracks to report for embarkation. I had slept through it all.

Our commanding officer was Dublin-born Paddy O'Daly, one of the outstanding soldiers of the War of Independence. Known to all of us as 'the Brig', he was of strong and forceful personality and possessed of unquestionable courage and ability as a leader of fighting men. He was wounded in 1916, and pre-1919 had spent periods in prison and internment. Michael Collins got him out of prison; he wanted him on active service outside. O'Daly reached the zenith of a remarkable army career with his appointment as GOC Kerry Command on 2 January 1923. His second in command of the force on board the *Lady Wicklow* was Commandant James McGuinness. Vice-Commandant James Dempsey was third in command. All three were wounded in Kerry. McGuinness was hit in the head in an ambush near Barraduff, on the road from Killarney to Rathmore. Dempsey lost an eye in an action at Kilgobnit, south of Killorglin, and was briefly held prisoner by the Republicans. O'Daly was wounded in the thigh at Kilcummin.

I recall that there were three Oriel House officers attached to our force. They were Commandant (later Colonel) Dave Neligan, and Captains James MacNamara and James Guiney. Neligan and MacNamara had pre-Truce service of the utmost importance as double agents working inside Dublin Castle and reporting direct to Collins, at whose express instructions they had joined us. Neligan had been sworn into the British secret service.

No doctor accompanied the expedition. The senior medical orderly with us was Sergeant T.J. (Ted) Keatinge from Drogheda.

It has been written that we were an elite force of the Dublin Guards, but so splendid a description should not lead to the idea that we were akin to those legendary British soldiers who, by tradition, died with their boots clean. It was good fighting material of approximate battalion strength, most of it tested pre-Truce or in the fighting in Dublin against the Republicans. Some of the men were recent recruits who had answered the call to arms issued by the Provisional Government, but our number also included IRA men who, having stood aside and remained non-partisan since the split, now decided to throw in their lot with the Free State Army. Very few of the unit, if any, were raw recruits in terms of experience, and not all were Dublin men. All the officers were IRA, men who had given notable service in the War of Independence.

Towards midday on 1 August, as the swell and sweep of the sea caused the *Lady Wicklow* to heave and roll, 450 or so army stomachs heaved and rolled with her. The misery was total and is an abiding memory with me. To step on to a companionway to a lower deck was to slither on vomit into an abyss of lost souls down below, most of them having their first taste of what the sea has to offer and what it expects back in return. I spent long hours leaning over the rails, keeping my mind diverted from the unpleasantness of life on board by watching the porpoises that tumbled and dived in the white wash churned up by the ship as she ploughed through rough water off the east coast.

At some hour in the pre-dawn of 2 August, I was roused from sleep by Commandant Neligan. He asked me what I knew of Fenit and Tralee town and district generally. I said I knew that whole area intimately. He then told me to report to Brigadier O'Daly in his cabin. This was a surprise command, but no cause for concern. As a corporal reporting to my commanding officer, I did not feel overwhelmed. Relationships between ranks in that embryo age of the Free State Army were free from the military stiffness of later years. Anyway, I had no qualms as to my ability to give information about the roads to be taken, the location of military and police barracks and other places. Four years had passed since I was last in Tralee, but time does not readily wipe the picture of youthful days from the screen of the mind.

I went to the Brigadier's cabin, knocked and was admitted at once. He was alone and seated, looking over a large map spread on a sea desk. He smiled a greeting that put me completely at ease, and I was soon talking away to him without a thought for his notable fighting record. I was surprised to learn from him that I was the only person on board with a knowledge of Fenit and Tralee. He questioned me and, using the map, told me to point out the routes we should take from Fenit to Tralee, the capture of which was our objective.

First, I told him about Fenit pier and its installations, extending for some 600 yards from the village straight out to the Great Samphire Island and then bearing east to the 250 yards of berthage facing the shore. I knew that railway tracks ran the entire length of the pier and that ships of up to 5,000 tons unloaded directly on to waggons; I suggested that if there were railway waggons on the pier, some 300 yards of which was a wooden viaduct, they would provide useful cover for troops advancing to take the village. I also told him that there was a coastguard station, a custom-house, a railway station and a police barracks, features that could be identified on the map. It did not cross my mind at the time that if the viaduct were mined and blown up it would be well nigh impossible for us to reach the shore, nor did I give a thought as to whether we carried engineering or bridging equipment. In fact, there was no such equipment on board. We learned our soldiering the hard way.

I showed the Brigadier where the pier joined the village road that leads the seven miles or so to Tralee, past Kilfenora railway station and through the Spa, a small seaside village about half way to our objective. The road, bounded on one side by the Tralee and Fenit railway line, leads directly into the town at Pembroke Street; on the other side, the shore bordering Tralee Bay comes close to the entrance by Strand Road. Both of these points of entry were important to the plan for the capture of the town as prepared by O'Daly and his senior officers later in the morning. Of equal importance was the railway line that runs to the north of Ballymullen military barracks for a mile or so, on the way from Tralee station to Killarney. On the far side of the town from the two points of entry mentioned are the Boherbee and Ballymullen districts. I knew there was a building in Boherbee that was known as the staff barracks, which had been used as married quarters by the British Army. In my view it was not of importance. The military barracks in Ballymullen was important, and I told the Brigadier that its distance from Fenit was almost nine miles. Looking at the map with him and considering the various routes skirting the town, I suggested that it would not be difficult to encircle the place and perhaps capture the military barracks together with its occupants if the landing at Fenit were deferred until after dark that night. His reply was that he had orders to take Tralee by noon.

Brigadier O'Daly said he was pleased with our discussion; the information would help him considerably in working out his plan for the landing at Fenit and the encircling of the Republican positions in Tralee. Before leaving his cabin I asked him if I might join the Dublin Guards. I told him the reason why I had joined the Army Medical Corps but that I had now given up hope of getting back to pharmacy. I also mentioned that I had been a pre-Truce member of C Company, 2nd Battalion Dublin Brigade IRA. This, I knew, would please him. He had at one time been a member of the battalion and it was very dear to his heart. He accepted me at once and said I could now consider myself one of the Guards. So there it was. His word was law and there were no transfer formalities or encumbering paperwork. Years later, I learned from Sergeant de Vere of Personnel Records at GHQ that, as I had disappeared from my Medical Corps unit 'without notice or trace', I had been entered as a deserter in my records sheet, a description with which I could find no reasonable grounds for disagreement.

When I was leaving the cabin, O'Daly said that as I was now a member of the Guards I should attach myself to the main body entering Tralee and act as guide where necessary. My feeling of elation was subdued by the thought that a guide leads from the front.

In consultation with his senior officers, O'Daly drew up this general plan for Fenit and Tralee:

1. Troops would disembark and rapidly advance along the pier to capture Fenit village.
2. After reassembly in Fenit, the main body would advance without delay under the command of Commandant J. McGuinness.
3. At the Spa a column under Captain W. McClean would detach and proceed along by the shore to Strand Road and enter the town at that point. This column would also detach a force to encircle the town, first by Blennerville to cut off any retreating Republican troops and then move round by Ballyard to make contact eventually with troops under Vice-Commandant J. Dempsey who were to engage in an encircling movement on the opposite side of the town.
4. The main force under Commandant J. McGuinness, with Captain J. (Sonny) Conroy as his second in command, would enter the town at Pembroke Street, having detached the encircling force under Vice-Commandant Dempsey for the advance along by the railway line towards the workhouse and by Workhouse Road to Ballymullen barracks.

5. Commandant McGuinness, having advanced from Pembroke Street and got through Rock Street, would make contact with Captain McClean's troops in the vicinity of the Square and Bridge Street, and from there the combined force would advance by the Mall and Castle Street to Moyderwell Cross, to capture the staff barracks and Ballymullen barracks.

Except for a diversion at Rock Street, which was of considerable tactical value, the general plan was carried out as devised. I don't know of any alternative plan that O'Daly might have had in mind before he found that I had intimate knowledge of the ground. As a matter of fact, unknown to him and to me, there was another soldier on board who knew Fenit and Tralee as well as I did, and probably better. He was a native of the town, Sergeant Jack Lydon of James's Street. Years afterwards, one of the senior officers with the expedition told me that O'Daly simply intended to get ashore at Fenit, march on Tralee and take the town, possibly with the assistance of a local pro-Treaty unit. The 18-pounder field piece and the armoured car would have been used against fortified opposition. Even with such armament the task would have been formidable and could not have been achieved by the force at his disposal were it not for the fact that circumstances in Kerry were greatly in his favour, although he was unaware of this at the time.

O'Daly had no knowledge of the strength and disposition of the forces that would oppose him. He knew that, in the main, the three Kerry IRA brigades were against the Treaty, to some extent out of loyalty to Austin Stack, who was one of its most bitter opponents. He had been led to believe, however, that he would be met at Fenit by Eamon Horan and some of his comrades of the IRA in Tralee who, like Horan himself, remained loyal to GHQ and were therefore in favour of the Treaty. There were no grounds for such optimism. Horan, an extraordinarily brave and valued pre-Truce member of the IRA, had never held a command. He had filled a roving commission during the War of Independence. It followed that he had no organized local group of pro-Treaty IRA men to support his own declaration for Michael

Collins and the 'stepping-stone' to a republic — a declaration
that he made openly in Tralee, even while the town was held
by the Republicans. To be a factor in assisting the landing
at Fenit he would have needed sufficient armed strength to
attack and subdue the Republican garrison in the coastguard
station, an action that should have synchronized with the arrival
of the *Lady Wicklow*. As he had no contact whatsoever with
the Free State Army GHQ prior to the Fenit landing, he knew
nothing of the overall plan for the sea-borne landings of troops
in the rear of the Republican positions in Munster. After we
had reached Tralee, he and local men who shared his views
made contact with us and assisted our troops. Within a few
days he had recruited and organized a column of Kerrymen
who formed part of the Free State Army in Kerry throughout
the remainder of the Civil War.

Having regard to the imponderables, O'Daly was fortunate
in finding a soldier on board the ship, in the person of myself,
who knew Fenit and Tralee intimately and could help him
with that knowledge. After my meeting with him I went back
on deck and rejoined my immediate comrades. It was the end
of surmise as to the objective of our mission. Word spread
rapidly throughout the ship that we were Fenit bound.

The morning mist had lifted and the sun shone on a calm
blue sea, unfolding the magnificent panorama of Tralee Bay.
Steaming ahead, we were still some distance from Fenit, which
is situated on the north-east corner of the entrance to the bay.
There was a great air of expectation among the troops. Some
were resting on deck, their heavy weapons and accoutrements
beside them. Others were gazing over the sides of the ship
at the splendour of the Kerry mountains and the great sweeps
of sandy beach. Who could have known the thoughts of these
soldiers, some of whom would die in so very short a time.

I looked from the starboard side and could see the tiny
uninhabited island of Inis Tuaisceart a mile north of which,
at 4.15 in the evening of Holy Thursday 1916, Captain Karl
Spindler brought the German arms ship, the auxiliary cruiser
Libau, disguised as the Norwegian freighter *Aud* for the gun-
running. There he cast anchor, right on time and in accordance

with his orders, after a voyage of incredible daring and hazard. But he was not expected until Sunday and so there was no pilot to meet him, nor were the Kerry Volunteers mobilized to receive and distribute the arms. The upshot was that, despite the superb seamanship of Spindler and through no fault of the Kerry Volunteers, the mission which had come so near to success ended in failure. To this day, the consignment that was to arm the Volunteers of the south and west lies at the bottom of the sea, somewhere near the entrance to Cork Harbour. Distantly, from the port side, I could see the golden sands of Banna strand where some ten hours after the arrival of the *Aud* off Inis Tuaisceart, Roger Casement had been put ashore from a German submarine.

As we moved ahead towards Tralee Bay on that August morning long ago, the quirks of history were truly there among us, from the German arms ship and the tragedy of Casement, the 'blood sacrifice' of Easter Week and the glorious years of national unity during the War of Independence. Now, a mere six years since the noble Proclamation of the Irish Republic, we had the greatest tragedy of our times, the 'blood of brothers combat', inspired less by ideology for a cause than by pride and adherence to individual leadership.

The *Lady Wicklow* steamed steadily towards Fenit. Very soon we would reach the danger point of recognition from the shore. 'All troops below deck,' rang out an order. Before going below I gave a quick last look over the beautiful and once familiar coastline, from Banna strand across the bay to the sands of Derrymore and Camp and Castlegregory, to the great vista of the Dingle peninsula reaching up towards the summit of mighty Mount Brandon.

Fenit, as I knew it from my boyhood, was a busy port of call for ships of fine tonnage bringing coal, timber, cement, bricks, slates, flour, grain, salt and general cargo to the merchant houses of Kerry. The ships came from far-away places, the ports of North and South America, Scandanavia, Archangel of Tzarist Russia, Rotterdam, Antwerp and from harbours as near as Liverpool and Limerick. The merchandise was off-loaded on to railway waggons on the pier, or on to barges that navigated the tidal canal to the wharfs known as 'the Basin' in Tralee. During the 1914-1918 war, British naval patrol boats came through the canal to the dry-dock at the Basin for cleaning and refitting. In 1922, the village consisted of some rows of houses — Harbour View and Samphire Terrace — a sprinkling of detached and semi-detached private houses, the usual village shops, a hotel, a couple of pubs, the railway station, the coastguard station, the custom-house, the police barracks and the post-office.

I have happy memories of travelling with my boyhood friends on the mid-week and Sunday excursion trains run by the Tralee and Fenit Railway Company from Tralee to Fenit, with intervening stops at the Spa and Kilfenora. On fine days, the trains carried capacity crowds out for a day's enjoyment at that delightful spot. They carried me there and brought me back for six old pennies, less than 3p. For another old penny a slot machine at the railway station would yield a bar of Nestles chocolate. What remained of a shilling (twelve old pennies) was sufficient to buy lemonade and biscuits or fruit, or *duillisc* and periwinkles from the traders who set up their stalls near the stile that one passes over when on the way to the beaches. The wares were displayed on spotless white sheets spread over common farm carts, the motive power for which grazed contentedly nearby.

In the summer of 1922, a small detachment of Republican troops from the 1st (Tralee) and 7th (Castleisland) Battalions Kerry No 1 Brigade took up precautionary garrison duties in Fenit on the orders of Brigadier Humphrey Murphy. They occupied the coastguard station once garrisoned by British marines whose duties were of a similar nature, for a different reason. Their commander was Tommy Sheehy, Captain of E Company (Oakpark) 1st Battalion. He had with him Seamus O'Connor, a 7th Battalion senior officer, who was appointed to the General Headquarters Staff at Fermoy after a few weeks in Fenit. From the vantage point of their post, the troops could observe the village and the activities of the people. They could also keep watch on the great pier stretching out below them to the Harbour Master's office and thence veering east to the berthage. From the berthing area to the shore measures some

700 yards across the water.

The garrison, as the unit of Republican troops came to be known, consisted of some twenty men armed with rifles and the usual complement of grenades and explosives; a machine-gun also, according to some accounts. Later, the garrison was supplemented by troops from the Fenit district. Mick Moriarty, Captain of the Churchill Company, was in charge of these local men. It was not of itself a formidable defence force, but its positioning and the nature of its assignment, which included the demolition of a large section of the wooden viaduct in the event of a military necessity, constituted serious opposition to a landing of troops. It is true to say that a mine beneath the viaduct was the corner-stone of the defence. Once the mine was exploded and a substantial part of the viaduct destroyed, no military force with accompanying heavy support equipment could hope to get ashore in effective strength rapidly enough for a surprise inland assault.

The men of the garrison were not particularly welcome in Fenit, then a place of quiet industry where fishermen plied their trade and others attended to the port services or to the needs of visitors. They were from the hinterland for the most part and therefore strangers by the standard of local judgement. Besides, they carried arms and moved about in a manner alien to the little village community.

By mid-July the spread of the Civil War following the Four Courts surrender had become the principal subject of talk and speculation even in this peaceful place so remote from the fighting. Could the war come to Fenit? It was a question that nobody could answer, but one that most of the village people thought about and put to friends and neighbours in the homes and in the pubs. The fighting seemed far enough away in Limerick and Waterford; it was well known that strong detachments of troops from the Kerry brigades had been sent to reinforce the Republicans in Limerick, Tipperary and Waterford.

As days went by and newspapers published alarming war news, the people of Fenit began to experience a greater sensitivity towards things around them. They feared an upheaval that would disturb the peace of their community.

And so, while the Republicans occupying the coastguard station were observing activities off shore and in the village, the Fenit people were by no means unaware of what the members of the garrison were doing. One thing the people had seen with alarm was the placing of the mine that threatened the pier. It was positioned beneath the wooden viaduct, two pylons out from the shore, and wired to a post-office telephone line which, in turn, was connected to an exploder at a point close to where Clifford's Hotel now stands. This was an act that gave rise to much talk and it intensified the sense of unease amongst all sections of the community, for it clearly signified that the viaduct would be blown up if danger from the sea at Fenit threatened the Republican positions in Kerry — and with the pier would go their lifeline to employment.

Men whose work was mainly connected with servicing the ships that continued to arrive in the port were well informed about the vast destruction of roads, railway lines and bridges in areas affected by the Civil War, as reported in the newspapers. They were concerned that Fenit pier could be in line for demolition. The men took action. On the night of Thursday, 27 July, they held a meeting that continued late into the following morning. They knew that notification of the arrival of a ship from Limerick next day had been received at the office of the Harbour Master, Robert McCarthy. They also knew that the garrison was easy on discipline and that the mine beneath the viaduct was not guarded. At 04.00 hours, two Harbour Board employees went stealthily to the pier and one of them cut the section of cable that connected the telephone line to the mine. Their action was totally apolitical, dictated by a bread-and-butter issue, the repercussions of which, from a military standpoint, were not their concern. The names of the two men were given to me, but their identity must not be disclosed.

Nobody had bothered to keep check on the vital piece of cable.

3

THE REORGANIZATION OF THE
KERRY NO 1 BRIGADE

O'Daly prepared his plan for the landing of his force at Fenit and the capture of Tralee in the expectation of stiff resistance. He was, of course, unaware of a number of factors that would greatly facilitate the task. These were: (1) the decision that had committed some of the best and most experienced fighting men in Kerry units to holding sectors of the Limerick–Waterford 'defence line', to the general neglect of Kerry coastal defence; (2) slackness in the Kerry No 1 Brigade staff, especially the failure to appreciate the probability, as distinct from the possibility, of a sea-borne landing of Free State troops at a port in the brigade area; (3) the dissension in the brigade and its crippling effect on the Tralee battalion (Commandant John Joe Sheehy's command); (4) the failure of the Fenit garrison to maintain proper vigilance while on war duty in a vital area, which failure permitted (5) the cutting of the cable to the mine that would have demolished a section of Fenit pier.

On Sunday, 30 July, two days before the Fenit bound *Lady Wicklow* headed out from the Liffey with Brigadier O'Daly's Dublin Guards on board, a crucial meeting of officers of Kerry No 1 Brigade was held in Castleisland. It had been summoned in a belated attempt to settle a divisive situation that was seriously interfering with the efficiency of the brigade and crippling the 1st (Tralee) Battalion. Commandant-General Liam Deasy travelled from his headquarters at Buttevant, County Cork, to preside at the meeting.

This issue had a vital bearing on the strength of the opposition to the landing at Fenit. To get to the heart of the matter, one must trace developments from December 1920, when Andy Cooney, a native of Ballyphillip, Nenagh, County Tipperary, was sent to Kerry by IRA General Headquarters as organizer attached to Kerry No 2 Brigade under Brigade Commander Humphrey Murphy.

Cooney, a medical student at University College, Dublin, had his study of medicine temporarily relegated to second place in his priorities by his commitment to the IRA. Prior to his posting in Kerry he had considerable experience of action, first in his native north Tipperary and subsequently with C Company, 3rd Battalion Dublin Brigade, as a member of which he had taken part in the smashing of the British ring of undercover agents in the city on 'Bloody Sunday', 21 November 1920. In April 1921, he was ordered by General Headquarters to transfer from Kerry No 2 Brigade to Kerry No 1 and take over command of the brigade from Commandant Paddy Cahill. This coincided with a general reorganization of the IRA that began with the formation of the 1st Southern Division (the first divisional unit established) at a meeting attended by officers of Cork and Kerry brigades at Kippagh, near Millstreet, County Cork on 26 April. All brigades were about to become linked in divisions. The 1st Southern then comprised nine brigades: Cork three, Kerry three, Waterford two and west Limerick one. Liam Lynch was appointed Divisional Commandant and Florence O'Donoghue Adjutant, the only two appointments made at the meeting. All three Cork brigades were represented. Kerry No 1 by Andy Cooney, and Kerry No 2 by Humphrey Murphy and John Joe Rice. Kerry No 3 was not represented, nor were the Waterford and West Limerick brigades. The three divisions formed prior to the Truce — the 1st and 2nd Southern and the 4th Northern — existed only on paper at that time.

The dismissal of Paddy Cahill as OC Kerry No 1 and his replacement by Cooney caused a great deal of friction, especially in Tralee. He was a popular local man and a member of Dáil Éireann and had been closest to Austin Stack in the lead-up to Easter Week 1916. When the regiment gave way to three Kerry brigades in 1917, he accepted the command of Kerry No 1. His second-in-command was Joe Melinn, Tralee, and other members of his staff were: Adjutant, Dan Sullivan, Tralee; Quartermaster, William (Billy) Mullins, Tralee; Intelligence Officer, Jim Kennedy, Annascaul. Cahill and his active service

column operated mainly from various headquarters in the
Dingle peninsula, locations that were not well chosen because
of their isolation in the western part of the brigade area,
especially as communications were very difficult in the
circumstances of those days. IRA General Headquarters was
dissatisfied with Kerry No 1 and ordered Cahill to be replaced
by Cooney.

In the Cahill Memorial Park in Tralee an engraved statue
bears testimony to the esteem and affection in which Paddy
Cahill's memory is held, and by none more than the people
of the Strand Road area, where he lived at Caherina for many
years.

Con Casey, a staff officer in the 1st (Tralee) Battalion at
the time when the general reorganization of the IRA began,
has recorded that he first met Andy Cooney on 11 July 1921,
the day the Truce became effective, when Cooney walked into
Tralee from west Kerry, accompanied by two local IRA officers,
Mick Fleming and Paddy Barry, both of D (Rock Street)
Company, 1st Battalion. 'Next day he asked me to be his
adjutant and I accepted,' Casey continued. 'Despite my being
a battalion officer, I had no knowledge of what was afoot in
the brigade. Indeed, Cooney was introduced to me as "Jack
Browne" and as such I knew him for some time afterwards.
He was a good organizer and a strict disciplinarian, and
physically he was a fine looking man!'

At the commencement of the Truce, Kerry No 1 Brigade
comprised six battalions: 1st (Tralee), OC John Joe Sheehy;
2nd (Ardfert), OC Tommy Clifford; 3rd (Lixnaw), OC Tom
Kennelly; 4th (Castlegregory), OC Tadhg Brosnan; 5th
(Dingle), OC Mick Moriarty, and 6th (Listowel), OC Paddy
Landers.

Commandant of the 1st Battalion, John Joe Sheehy, was
appointed to the post in November 1920 by Paddy Cahill,
then OC Kerry No 1. He succeeded Michael Doyle, a much
older man, to whom he had been Vice-Commandant. In fact,
he had been Acting Commandant for some time previous to
his appointment. Battalion Adjutant was Jerry Hanafin and
the Quartermaster was Mattie Moroney.

The battalion consisted of three companies — A, B and

D. A Company drew its membership from Boherbee, Ballymullen, Moyderwell, Upper Castle Street and related areas; Jack Dowling was Company Captain. Such was the influence of John Joe Sheehy in the Boherbee area, however, that it was impossible to separate him from the command of A Company. As put by one old comrade, 'Even after he became Battalion OC his word remained law in the company.'

B Company drew from Strand Road, Spa Road, Caherina, Basin View, James's Street and related areas; Dan Jeffers, a Strand Road man was Company Captain. D Company drew from Rock Street, Pembroke Street, Bridge Street, Balloonagh, Gallows Field and related areas; Company Captain was John O'Connor, a shoemaker, of Upper Rock Street. He was one of seven brothers, all Volunteers, and all but he were railway men. C Company, which once drew membership from the town centre, including men whose employment was in that sector, had ceased to exist, its members dispersed among other companies.

The battalion's three town companies had associate rural companies, officially known as E, F, G and H, although these letters were rarely used. A Company had close association with E Company — Farmer's Bridge and Ballyseedy (Johnny Duggan, Company Captain, assisted by Johnny Connor), and with Ballybeggan and Oakpark (Tommy Sheehy and Tom Talbot); B Company was closely linked with H Company — the Kerries and Blennerville (Jimmy O'Shea), as was D Company with G Company — Doon and Ballyroe (Batt Dowling and John McDonnell). Men of these rural companies were generally regarded as members of the associate town companies.

The commandants of the Ardfert, Lixnaw and Dingle battalions were replaced by Paddy O'Connor, Paddy O'Mahony of Ballydonoghue and Jim Sullivan of Kinard, respectively. Paddy Landers retired as OC Listowel Battalion and was replaced by Jim Sugrue. Landers, a Tralee man, was a whitesmith with the Listowel and Ballybunion Railway Company of Listowel, which operated the unique single rail system between Listowel and Ballybunion. Sugrue's native place was Cahirciveen. He was employed in the drapery

business in Listowel. Tom Kennelly, the displaced commandant of the Lixnaw Battalion, had been a RIC constable; he
had resigned from the force in sympathy with the independence
movement. The new Dingle Battalion Adjutant was Gregory
Ashe, brother of the illustrious Tomas Ashe of Kinard who
died on 25 September 1917 as the immediate result of brutal
ill treatment while on hunger-strike in Mountjoy jail. Michael
Harrington was Dingle Company Captain.

The new Kerry No 1 Brigade staff was: OC, Humphrey
Murphy, Ballybeg, Currow, Castleisland; Vice-OC, Tomas
O Donnachadha, Reenard, Cahirciveen; Adjutant, Con Casey,
Bridge Street, Tralee; Quartermaster, Maurice Fleming, Gas
Terrace, Tralee; Engineer, Jim Flavin, Lower Rock Street,
Tralee; Medical Officer, Dr. Roger O'Connor, Listowel;
Signals, Ned Moriarty, Blennerville, Tralee; Intelligence, Sean
Hyde, Toureen, west Cork, and Mattie Ryan, Boher, Killaloe,
County Clare.

In the early days of the Truce, Commandant Cooney moved
his headquarters from west Kerry to a more suitable location
at Ardfert, some six miles north-west of Tralee, and from
there he proceeded to reorganize the brigade. 'The reorganization resulted in a tremendous shake up,' Con Casey recalled.
In some areas the displacement of Paddy Cahill was bitterly
resented, as was the subsequent ousting of his entire brigade
staff. B Company of the 1st (Tralee) Battalion refused to co-
operate with Cooney. Tadhg Brosnan, Commandant of the
4th (Castlegregory) Battalion, was ambivalent out of loyalty
to Cahill, but held his command. The brigade remained intact,
however, except for the dissidence in the 1st Battalion.

Brigade training camps were set up at Ardfert and
preparations put in train for a probable resumption of hostilities
with the British. Divisional Commandant Liam Lynch,
accompanied by Commandant Liam Deasy, his Vice-OC, came
to Ardfert and inspected the camps.

Cooney became ill in the autumn of 1921 and had to return
to Dublin for medical treatment. Commandant Humphrey
Murphy, OC Kerry No 2 Brigade, was then ordered by General
Headquarters to take over from him as OC Kerry No 1, and
he was succeeded in the command of Kerry No 2 by his Vice-

Commandant, John Joe Rice of Bonance, Kenmare. In this way the reorganization brought Murphy's native battalion, Castleisland, into Kerry No 1 as the 7th Battalion, with Jerh O'Leary of Scartaglin the OC. An 8th (Ballylongford) Battalion was formed and Con Dee was appointed OC. The departure of Cooney in no way altered the situation in the Tralee Battalion. B Company of at least 200 men continued to give its absolute loyalty to Paddy Cahill and refused to serve under Humphrey Murphy. As well as seriously impairing the efficiency of the brigade, the divisiveness gave rise to a great deal of bitterness in the battalion area. Cahill men and Murphy men were passing one another in the streets of Tralee without as much as a nod of greeting — men who had known one another all their lives.

On 9 February 1922, units of the 1st Battalion took over Ballymullen military barracks and the building called the staff barracks in Boherbee from the departing British. Ballymullen barracks had been regimental district headquarters of the Royal Munster Fusiliers since July 1881. British military posts elsewhere in Kerry were taken over about the same time by local IRA units. The RIC vacated all their barracks in the county a little later. Wherever possible, IRA maintenance parties were put into the vacated military barracks and the more important RIC barracks.

In March 1922, Con Casey left his posting on the staff of Kerry No 1 Brigade to go as Adjutant 1st Eastern Division at the request of Andy Cooney, who had been appointed Divisional OC, with headquarters in Millmount military barracks, Drogheda.

Following the appointment of Liam Lynch as Chief of Staff of the Republican Army on 9 April 1922, Liam Deasy succeeded him as OC 1st Southern Division and also became Deputy Chief of Staff, with headquarters at Buttevant. Keenly concerned about the continuing divisive situation in the Tralee Battalion, Kerry No 1, Deasy made the journey to Castleisland for the officers' meeting on Sunday, 30 July, determined on ending the dissension that persisted as virulently as ever in the fifth week of the Civil War. He presided at the meeting, which was attended by Humphrey Murphy and his staff, and by the former Commandant Paddy Cahill and some of the dissident battalion officers. It was a strenuous session and its outcome a compromise in the formation of a 9th Battalion which was mainly B Company of the 1st Battalion, given a new status and a new name. Paddy Paul Fitzgerald was appointed Commandant and Paddy Garvey Vice-Commandant. No other appointment was made.

The new battalion, which would draw its manpower from the former B Company area and related areas that included Ballyard, Barrow, Blennerville, Churchill, Derrymore, Fenit, the Kerries and the Spa, was made accountable for the coastal defence of the Tralee district. Fenit was the most important point in its area of responsibility.

Commandant Fitzgerald, well aware of the need for urgency in establishing the effectiveness of his new command, held a meeting of his officers in Tralee on Monday, 31 July. The most important decision to emerge from the meeting was that the new battalion would take over Fenit port and village from the garrison in the coastguard station on the following Sunday, 6 August. Events were to prove that the timing was four days late.

Paddy (Nap) Daly, OC 1st (Tralee) Battalion Fianna Éireann, was closely associated with B Company, 1st (Tralee) Battalion, IRA, which had just become the 9th Battalion of Kerry No 1 Brigade. Fianna Éireann as such had no involvement in the formation, or otherwise, of the 9th Battalion. Daly was instructed by Paddy Paul Fitzgerald to take an urgent dispatch and a verbal message to Liam Deasy at Buttevant military barracks, requesting the immediate return to Tralee of a column of Kerry troops led by Tadhg Brosnan, Commandant of the 4th Battalion, then believed to be in the Bruff, Bruree and Kilmallock sector of County Limerick, where heavy fighting was taking place.

There was no motor transport available and Daly had to travel to Buttevant by an early morning train from Tralee: 'It was the first of August and I was accompanied by Jackie Price, who was also a member of the newly formed battalion,' Daly has recorded. 'He came from Millstreet to work at the Munster Warehouse in Tralee, and as he knew north Cork as only a native can he was a good man to have as guide in case I had difficulty in locating General Deasy. It so happened that we were kept waiting a long time in Buttevant barracks before we met the General, and even then, for reasons best known to himself, he did not immediately disclose his identity to us. When he had read the dispatch, he told us that due to the fluid nature of the fighting in the region of County Limerick, where Brosnan's column was engaged, and also because of the difficulty that he had in maintaining contact with his forces, he did not know exactly where to find the column. He did promise to have the message conveyed to Brosnan as quickly as possible. We had to be satisfied with that.'

Daly's next problem was to get Price and himself back to Tralee: 'There was no transport available and we had to remain overnight in Buttevant. Next morning we took a train to Cork city, hoping to get from there to Tralee in a lorry that Mattie Moroney had driven from Tralee to Cork with a load of bicycles for Cork No 1. When we arrived in Cork we went straight to Victoria barracks.' The first man they met there was Jim Flavin of Tralee, the Engineer Officer attached to Kerry No 1 headquarters staff. 'What on earth are you doing here,' he asked, 'or don't you know the Staters have landed at Fenit?' Daly and Price were dumbfounded. In Daly's own words: 'We felt that if the Staters had landed in force there was no way that our available men could prevent them from taking Tralee and overunning the whole county.'

As an instance of how families were divided on the Treaty issue, it should be mentioned that while Jim Flavin was a brigade engineer in the Republican Army, his brother Jack was one of the group of local officers known as 'the Dandy Six' on the Free State side.

Finding transport from Cork to Tralee turned out to be more of a problem than Paddy Daly had anticipated. Moroney's lorry was owned by Murphy Brothers of Cork, butter and egg buyers for the Manchester Co-operative Wholesale Society's branch in Pembroke Street, Tralee.

'One of the Murphys was an officer in Cork No 1,' Daly continued, 'and I went to a brigade meeting to contact him about borrowing the lorry to get us back to Tralee. He told me he had to hold the lorry in Cork. I understood his attitude, as transport was scarce and precious, but I said we would have to commandeer a means of transport to Tralee immediately because of the Free State landing at Fenit. He then relented and had his own driver take Moroney, Price and me as far as Killarney, but no further. From there the driver returned to Cork with the lorry.' From Killarney the three from Tralee set out to join their units in such areas as Ballymacelligott and Derrymore.

Although the 1st Southern Division was anti-Treaty it did not follow that all officers and men of the division took the Republican side in the Civil War. Some senior officers and others with distinguished service in the Anglo-Irish war remained neutral. Many joined the Free State Army.

In *No Other Law*, his biography of Liam Lynch, Florence O'Donoghue gives the strength of the three Kerry brigades as: No 1 — 4,000; No 2 — 3,400, and No 3 — 1,350; in all, 8,750 officers and men. Of these, approximately 1,000 were under arms on the Republican side at the outbreak of the Civil War, according to Staff Captain Mick McGlynn, who was in Ballymullen barracks when the Dublin Guards landed at Fenit. In conversation with me many years afterwards, John Joe Sheehy was in complete agreement with McGlynn that the Kerry combat troops who were engaged in the so-called Limerick–Waterford line were amongst the best available in the country.

There were four Kerry columns in various sectors of the 'line' and they included men who had fought at Lispole, Headford Junction, Glenbeigh, Castlemaine and in other actions against the British. There is no record of the combined strength of these units, but 250 would appear to be a reasonable estimate.

Con O'Leary, Quartermaster Kerry No 2, had men from his brigade and from the Listowel and Castleisland Battalions Kerry No 1 in his command in Limerick city, and subsequently in the Bruff, Bruree, Kilmallock triangle in County Limerick. Tom McEllistrim of Ballymacelligott, a senior officer with an impeccable Anglo-Irish war record, was in charge of the 7th Battalion Unit in the city. Tadhg Brosnan, OC Castlegregory Battalion, also had his Kerry No 1 column in the triangle. Paddy (Belty) Williams, a member of Tralee Battalion Fianna Éireann, who was with Brosnan, remembered that 'it was a small column of some twenty-five or thirty men, of whom seven were Tralee Fianna members: Billy Myles, Tommy (Nuts) Connor, Paddy Reidy, Paddy Williams, Andrew (Gundy) MacSweeney and Denis (Tucker) Healy of Ballyard.' In the main, the column was made up of men from the Tralee and West Kerry Battalions. Jerry Myles of A Company Tralee Battalion led a Kerry No 1 column which had several engagements with the Free State troops in County Tipperary sectors of the Lynch 'defence line' in the early days of the war. The men of his column were drawn mainly from the Tralee and North Kerry Battalions. About mid-July, the column was forced to surrender to a Free State Force led by Commandant Jerry Ryan and Mick Small at Raheelty, near Thurles, after a spirited rearguard action that went on for two hours. The fourth Kerry unit was engaged in the fighting in Waterford city and county.

4

FENIT COULD HAVE BEEN
OUR GALLIPOLI

The *Lady Wicklow* steamed in closer to land. There was no sign of recognition from the shore, although binoculars could easily pick out members of the crew and the covered deck cargo which, in fact, was the field-gun and the armoured car. The buildings at Fenit were now clearly distinguishable. As the Harbour Master's office knew nothing about us, there was no arrangement for pilotage or for our reception at the pier. Needless to say, such thoughts were not occupying our minds.

A canoe carrying three men was observed making towards us, two pulling at the oars. The ship slowed down, then stopped, and the canoe was brought alongside. The third man came on board. He was a local pilot, John Fitzgerald of Tawlaght. At first he had wondered about this unexpected visitor, a stranger to the port of Fenit, but after some hesitation he decided to meet her and had his sons Paddy and John row him out.

Once on board, Fitzgerald felt that there was something odd about the atmosphere. The crew seemed to be tense and uneasy. He asked what was beneath the great tarpaulins that covered the 'merchandise' on deck. 'Livestock and lead,' he was told, a reply that did nothing to ease the mind of a man who had already sensed strain and anxiety in those around him. Suddenly, hobnailed boots clattered on a companionway and a number of men emerged from below deck. Fitzgerald, to his consternation, saw that they were dressed in the uniform of officers of the Free State Army. It was all too much for him and he dashed to get back over the side and rejoin his sons, but they, completely unaware of the situation on board, were well on their way back to the shore. He was grabbed at once and peremptorily ordered to take the ship to anchorage at the pier. He had no choice but to do as ordered. Gently we got under way again. We were now inside Little Samphire Island and its lighthouse. All around us was a stillness and an apparent peace under the warm sun of that summer's morning.

Not surprisingly, there were no longshoremen to take the berthing lines at the pier head. The tide did not suit and the pilot's first approach failed. There was an irritating delay before a second and closer approach was made. This time, Sergeant Jack Lydon of Tralee, a brave and experienced soldier, jumped from the ship with a line and secured it to a bollard, thus facilitating the movement of the ship for berthing.

The *Lady Wicklow* came to anchor. The time was 10.30 on the morning of 2 August. All was noise and bustle on board as we assembled according to the units and assignments ordered by officers and NCOs. The ship towered above the pier, screening the activity from shore observation. Gang-planks were lowered. Their weapons at the ready, our leading groups had their orders: 'Ready! Out! Rush the pier and seize the village! Come on, move! Quickly! Quickly!' The orders were urgent and the response was immediate. Forward troops hurried down the gang-planks and dashed from the berthing area. They were on their way to the village.

The many and noisy activities centred on a ship that was not expected at the port went entirely unobserved by the Republican garrison. Not so by some employees of the Harbour Board. The longshoreman, Jim Moriarty, thought that there was 'something suspicious' about the ship when she was south of his house on the pier and he decided not to take the line for berthing. Another employee, Johnny Sheehan, who lived at 4 Samphire Terrace, was engaged in shepherding a flock of wayward goslings into the field called 'the pound' when he caught sight of the *Lady Wicklow*. She was then outside the entrance to Tralee Bay and making for Fenit. The pound was adjacent to the Republican post at the coastguard station. Sheehan had worked in Ramsgate, Kent, during the 1914-18 war and had seen many troop transports during his time there. Meeting an armed member of the garrison on the road, he remarked to him that the ship steaming in looked very like a transport. 'The Republican soldier was not impressed,' Sheehan recalled. 'At all events, he took no action.' Sheehan's opinion was based on 'the profile of the ship, which was unlike that of the usual cargo steamers calling at the port.' Besides, he knew, as did most people in Fenit, that there had been no notification to the harbour authorities or to the customs and excise officer of the arrival of any ship on that day.

Sheehan watched the strange ship as she rounded the pier and was brought to anchor; then he set out for the berthing area and a close inspection. He was well on his way from the village when he saw uniformed soldiers spilling from the ship and running along the pier. He knew at once that they could only be 'Staters'. In a state of high alarm, he turned and ran back to warn the village and alert the garrison in the coastguard station. Some members of the garrison were still in bed. Others were just lazily resting, perhaps wondering what the sunny summer's day would bring. Nobody was on the alert. Sheehan's news galvanized all of them into activity. Two who had charge of the mine tried to blow the viaduct. They raced from the coastguard station, across the track and over the wall and road to where the firing point was located. They quickly connected the detonator box to a length of cable that had been soldered to the telephone line. The rest should have been easy. All that remained was to press the plunger down and watch the resultant destruction of material created by both god and man. The plunger was slammed down, again and yet again, but nothing happened. The viaduct did not collapse. No soldier was killed. Had the Republicans succeeded in blowing the viaduct there was no way that we could have got ashore quickly, or at all, for we carried no bridging equipment, a strange omission, even allowing for the fact that we were then only in the embryo age of our organized military existence. It was extraordinary that an action by non-combatants, solely motivated by a bread-and-butter issue (as described in the preceding chapter) should have saved O'Daly and his Dublin Guards from a severe and costly reverse.

The reason for the failure to detonate the mine remained a subject of speculation until this day. Some thought it was due to an electrical fault. John Joe Sheehy believed that it was sabotage by a member of the garrison who changed sides after we had landed. It is only now that the facts are revealed, as given to me by a son of one of the men who cut the cable which connected the telephone line to the mine. No member of the garrison defected to us.

Reacting to the alarm raised by Johnny Sheehan, those of the village whose homes were in the immediate danger zone rushed to find safer quarters. Families cleared out as fast as their legs would carry them, one house being vacated in such haste that retired RIC Sergeant Gildea's pension was left at some risk on the kitchen table; in the urge to be gone while the going was good nobody had bothered about securing doors. 'A whole month's pension and a sizeable sum at that,' the Sergeant said with feeling after the household had ventured back, following the all-clear. To the intense relief of those concerned, not a penny of the money had been touched. Gildea's pension was still intact on the table where it had been abandoned in the flurry of departure.

Denis Sheehy was employed by the Tralee and Fenit Railway Company at Fenit station. He was looking through a window of the office and saw the *Lady Wicklow* coming into port. 'The tide was unsuitable,' he recalled, 'and the pilot had great difficulty in bringing her alongside. He was helped by Jack Lydon. If the berthing had not been delayed by the tide, an earlier landing of the Free Staters would have caught most of the Republicans in bed. As it was, they were unaware of what was happening until the soldiers were seen running from the ship towards the office of the Harbour Master, Robert McCarthy, situated at the angle where the pier turns north for the village. They expected a Free State landing and kept watch for it, but were taken by surprise in the end.'

John O'Mahony, son of the customs officer, was fifteen years of age at the time. He saw a rush of armed men pass his home in the custom-house, which was next to the coastguard station, and watched their mad scramble for any cover giving a field of fire to the pier and the ship berthed there, all of a thousand yards away. 'She was out of effective rifle range,' he recalled, 'and bullets spattered the sea. The men of the garrison had only .303 service rifles, but they opened fire on troops coming within range as the Staters advanced rapidly up the narrow pier, then only a passage. These troops were an easy concentrated target and some were seen to fall. They then took cover behind loose railway waggons that they started to push towards the village.' The garrison had instructed Denis Sheehy not to leave waggons on the pier, but some were left there overnight because he was unable to have them moved.

Firing from the Republican positions was brisk and some of our soldiers were wounded before they could take advantage of the protection afforded by harbour buildings and installations. With a roar, the Vickers gun of the armoured car, together with Lewis guns and rifles, opened up from the deck of the *Lady Wicklow* with terrifying effect. The Vickers gunner plastered the upper gable end of the coastguard station. This cover fire enabled troops to advance along the pier towards the village. Hundreds of yards of exposed straight and narrow pier lay ahead as our leading units dashed forward against what was expected to be the defensive positions of the Republicans, with the ever-present fear that an exploding mine would send us all sky-high, along with sections of the viaduct. Fortunately for us, there was no explosion, and the railway waggons gave protection. Soldiers got behind the waggons and pushed them almost as far as the railway station, then dashed forward, firing at selected targets.

The intensity of the gunfire from the *Lady Wicklow* made a lasting impression on William Crowley of Fenit, then a mere lad of fourteen years. 'The coastguard station caught the Staters' fire and was blasted,' he recalled, 'and the covered footbridge over the railway tracks was an interference with the garrison's field of fire, as were some houses near the entrance to the pier.' In his recollection of the eventful morning, 'the garrison, at the time of the landing, consisted of fifteen or, at most, twenty men from Tralee under Tommy Sheehy, and about six from the Fenit area whose immediate officer was Mick Moriarty.' Young Crowley and Denis Sheehan, who had watched the *Lady Wicklow* steam into port, were among a number of local civilians rounded up by our troops in the course of the morning. All were released after a few hours' detention. In the circumstances of the time it was often difficult to draw a line of recognition between combatant and non-combatant, as very few Republican troops were dressed in any kind of uniform.

Mary Sheehan (later Mrs Dan King), employed in the house of Robert McCarthy, the Harbour Master, had expected him home as usual for morning coffee at ten o'clock. He was a punctual man and regular in his habits. On this particular morning, thoughts of the coffee break were scattered by the sudden noise of the guns. Mary Sheehan and Olive McCarthy, daughter of the house, rushed to look through the south gable window, which commanded a view of the harbour. They saw that the pier was 'alive with soldiers'. Then they got binoculars for a better view. Bullets smashed into the wooden window frames, showering the girls with glass. Another smacked against the wall behind them. They hastily got down on the floor and said their prayers.

The postmistress, Mrs Brian Kelly, and members of her household were also saying their prayers. Located in Harbour View, a row of houses some fifty yards to the east of the pier entrance and a somewhat longer distance from the shore, the post-office was in no man's land, facing the berthing area and directly in the line of fire between the *Lady Wicklow* and the Republican positions. (There were no intervening buildings in 1922). Bullets ricochetted off the chimney, leaving marks that remain to this day. Post-office business was not a priority with Mrs Kelly that morning.

Fred McKibben, a native of Carrig Island near Ballylongford in north Kerry, had a coal and general merchant business at the Old Bridge in Fenit. He was in his office that morning taking a telephone call from John Mangan, a butter and egg merchant of Rock Street, Tralee. Their conversation was abruptly halted by McKibben. After a moment's pause he calmly told Mangan that intensive gunfire had just started in the direction of the pier. 'I think the Free State Army must be landing here,' he said. It was an eventuality that he had been anticipating. Mangan called out the sensational news to his staff, one of whom, Denis Keane of Caherina, was a member of the newly formed 9th Battalion of Kerry No 1 Brigade.

Keane jumped on a bike and sped away to alert his OC, Paddy Paul Fitzgerald.

McKibben's was the only report of the landing to reach Tralee direct from Fenit that morning.

Within minutes of our front units reaching the mainland, the railway station, the coastguard station and the police barracks were in our hands. Total surprise and speed of movement had made for rapid success. The garrison, devastated by the massive gunfire from the *Lady Wicklow,* had retreated without loss. They had no option but to withdraw from the coastguard station and other positions which, in fact, were no longer tenable. 'We beat a disorderly retreat,' one of them told me more than half a century afterwards. 'Back with us inland under cover given by Egan's *bohereen,* back towards Churchill. There were no plans for retreat, no plans to regroup.' Their dependence on the mine was such that they had no plan of any kind to meet the emergency that came in from the sea. They did regroup very quickly, however, and some of them took up positions in an old ring fort on a rise near Kilfenora village. The fort has long since been levelled to make way for housing.

Within half an hour of the ship's berthing, the first important foothold had been gained in the south, with its immediate threat to what remained of the Lynch 'defence line'. The fight for Fenit was over. It could so easily have gone otherwise. Fenit could have been our Gallipolli had the Republican leadership appreciated its importance relative to their Munster 'front'. The fact is that we ought never to have been allowed to land.

Almost without pause, our main body began to assemble in Fenit for the seven-mile march to Tralee. It was essential for us to keep moving ahead rapidly to minimize the time for the build-up of armed resistance inland, which, we felt, must follow news of the landing. Some troops were detached for the armoured car and the field piece, both of which were held up in the berthing area. The motor tow for the 18-pounder had been badly damaged at the landing and the armoured car was held back to protect the gun.

The sun was already high in the sky on that beautiful August morning. Somebody said it was a fine day to die for Ireland.

Timothy Egan was digging potatoes in a field near the road as we marched past. The field is now Marian Terrace, Fenit. In a moment of inspiration, Commandant Neligan approached him and asked if he had horses and ploughing tackle, including chains and traces. Egan said his father had. Taking some soldiers, Neligan went up to the farmhouse and got a horse and a mare named Dolly, as well as tackling and a common cart. Accompanied by Timothy Egan's brother Maurice (Mossy), they returned to where the 18-pounder was parked on the pier and, with the chains, set about tackling the cart to the gun. Dolly got excited and the gun crew were unable to handle the team. Mossy Egan then lent a hand. He tackled Dolly to the field-gun and the horse towed it on its own wheels, without the cart. Escorted by the armoured car and with Egan guiding his father's horse, the party moved off after the column of Dublin Guards.

Commandant Paddy Paul Fitzgerald of the 9th Battalion, Kerry No 1 Brigade, was at home at 1 Spa Road when Denis Keane came running in, breathless from excitement and exertion. 'The Staters are in Fenit,' Keane blurted out. Fitzgerald grabbed his bike and made for the police barracks in High Street, half a mile down Strand Road. The barracks, until recently an RIC stronghold, was the battalion assembly station. From there he telephoned the news to Ballymullen military barracks, headquarters of the 1st Battalion. 'It was the first they heard of the landing and their surprise was as great as mine,' Fitzgerald recalled. 'I was asked for details that I did not have, the tone of voice conveying more than a hint of disbelief. Fenit had not reported anything, and so Ballymullen felt it must be a false alarm.'

Ballymullen was to hear more about the landing within the space of a few minutes. Connie Gallagher, a young assistant in the Tralee general post-office in Edward Street, was on the phone to the Spa sub-post-office from her own exchange. To her astonishment, she was told that there was a battle going on at Fenit. 'The firing can be heard over here at the Spa,' said the voice at the other end of the line. 'There's shooting at Fenit!' Miss Gallagher exclaimed to her colleagues. At that, a Republican officer on duty in the exchange snatched the phone from her and heard direct from the Spa sub-postmistress that she was listening to the din of heavy firing at Fenit. He got on the line to Ballymullen barracks at once and confirmed the report already phoned in by Paddy Paul Fitzgerald. 'Surely to God, Fenit should have been first to raise the alarm,' Miss Gallagher heard him say. Ballymullen had been trying to raise Fenit on the phone, without success. In the Fenit sub-office, Mrs. Kelly was still sensibly intent on prayer and safety to the exclusion of all things earthly.

In Ballymullen barracks, recovery from the stunning surprise was rapid. Incredulity gave way to frantic activity. Acting Brigade Adjutant Eugene McCarthy took charge. Brigade OC Humphrey Murphy was at home in Ballybeg, some twelve miles south-west of Tralee, and a dispatch rider was sent out there to alert him. All available officers and men were called from their homes and from places of work in the factories, shops and fields, and directed to their assembly stations, as were members of Fianna Éireann and Cumann na mBan. The failure of Fenit telephone exchange was frustrating. Calls were still not being answered. It was decided to send out a senior officer to investigate the military situation.

Captain Mick McGlynn, recently posted to brigade head-quarters staff in Ballymullen barracks, was asleep in the officers' quarters. He had been out from midnight until seven o'clock that morning, in charge of a coast-watching patrol 'on the look out for any unusual activity between Ardfert, some six miles north-west of Tralee, and the County Limerick port of Foynes on the Shannon.' Apart from some activity by local Republican groups, the entire coastline was without protection, McGlynn recalled. Shortly after 10.30 o'clock he was roused by Eugene McCarthy and ordered to 'proceed immediately to Fenit to investigate a reported landing there by Free State troops, and to assess the situation.'

'I got ready at once,' McGlynn continued, 'and drove furiously towards Fenit in the only available car, a British military-type Crossley tender I had got my hands on when we took the main Free State Army position in Listowel on 30 June. Since then it was being used by the night patrol. I nursed possessive instincts towards that Crossley because while drivers were scarce in Kerry, transport of any kind was a damn sight more so.'

As he raced the tender over the rutted road to Fenit, raising grey clouds of limestone dust, McGlynn was inclined to reject the report of a landing, his mind on the mine beneath the viaduct. 'I hit the road only in spots with my Crossley,' he recalled, 'because time was not on our side if it was a fact that the Staters were ashore. But this I found hard to believe, for with the viaduct effectively demolished I felt that our twenty or more men in the village were sufficient for a holding operation until reinforced.'

McGlynn was not long in doubt about the situation: 'I left the Crossley about a mile short of the village and moved to a vantage point where I saw no sign of resistance by our men but every indication that a landing had been effected. The viaduct was intact and that explained a lot. I could not contact any member of the garrison.' By that time the Republican troops had evacuated their positions, and McGlynn could not see them from the coast road because they had retreated inland. He returned to the Crossley and 'drove like hell to Ballymullen barracks', no doubt in his mind as to the seriousness of the situation; he was convinced that the mine had been sabotaged. He reported his findings and was then ordered to take the Crossley to the police barracks, where he would collect men of the 9th Battalion and rush them towards Fenit.

It is indicative of the brigade's total failure to take effective action in an emergency to find that McGlynn, a fighting officer whose courage and capability had been proved in the war against the British, was in the hour of crisis merely assigned the duties of a transport driver. When he drew up his Crossley at the police barracks he 'found about fourteen of our troops ready and awaiting transport. Most of them belonged to the Strand Road Company [the core of the 9th Battalion] and Dan Jeffers was in charge. They quickly boarded the tender and we headed towards Fenit. Up Strand Road we went and I remember girls tossing packets of cigarettes and sweets to us during a brief stop at Spa Road.'

McGlynn was happy that the men of Strand Road were going into action, as 'their mettle' was well known to him. 'The tragedy was that they were so few,' he added. 'I had been a Strand Road Company man myself before I transferred to Kerry No 2 Brigade during the Tan war.'

Paddy Paul Fitzgerald, Paddy Garvey and some others of the 9th Battalion were minutes ahead of McGlynn's Crossley, tearing over the road to Fenit in Terence J. Liston's car. Liston was one of the few motor owners in Tralee and his car had been outside his law office in Denny Street, where his driver, Mike O'Brien, had parked it that morning. Fitzgerald had commandeered the car and Jack Barrett was now behind the wheel.

McGlynn pulled up at Oyster Hall, about half a mile on the Tralee side of Sammy's Rock, a strong vantage point rising high above the road some two miles distant from Fenit. Barrett and Liston's car were on the roadside, facing Tralee; Fitzgerald and his men were already out of sight. 'I dropped the boys and turned back to town for more,' McGlynn recalled. 'The few I had brought out did not stand a chance of holding up the Staters. I could see that there was no possibility of any sort of delaying action unless Tommy Sheehy's men made contact with Jeffers's lot and they jointly opposed the advance from favourable ground.'

Back in Tralee, McGlynn was told that no men could be spared to reinforce those already disputing the Free State advance. He was not altogether surprised by the decision. 'It must be understood,' he explained, 'that most members of our active service units were away fighting in Limerick, Waterford and Tipperary. Once the situation at Fenit was evaluated in Ballymullen, Tralee men reporting for duty were hastily assigned stations or other tasks in or near the town. Although we had approximately a thousand men under arms, very few seasoned soldiers were immediately available for a defence of Tralee.'

Former Brigadier Paddy Cahill reported at the 9th Battalion assembly station that morning and hurriedly selected defensive positions in the Strand Road sector. These included Lunham' house (now St Anne's flats). Another was the yard wall a the rear of the police barracks in High Street.

Henry Carrick of A Company, 1st Battalion, heard of the landing while talking to neighbours at the door of his home in Boherbee shortly before eleven o'clock that morning. He recalled that Company Captain Jack Dowling, who lived in Moyderwell, 'came running round the corner to our house' Carrick was 'thunderstruck' by the news he brought and so was everyone else within earshot. 'Jack shouted that the Staters were in Fenit. He left Mills bombs with me for delivery to Paddy Paul Fitzgerald and then away with him to alert other members of our own company. I took the bombs to B Company's assembly station at the old RIC barracks.'

News of the landing reached Jim O'Shea, Captain of H Company (Blennerville and the Kerries) at the Basin, where he was helping to unload general cargo from the *Flesk*, a lighter servicing the port of Tralee from Fenit Harbour. Batty O'Sullivan, captain of the *Flesk*, was left on his own with his partly unloaded lighter as the work force vanished in various directions, Jim O'Shea to 'No 1 barracks' [the RIC barracks], which was his assembly point. 'Paddy Cahill was in charge,' he recalled. 'With Jack McCarthy, Willie Murphy and some others I was detailed by him to take up positions in Lunham's house in Strand Road. Jack and I were at a window on the first floor overlooking the Dingle Railway tracks.'

Hanna O'Connor was at work as usual in the Rock Street commercial office of J.M. Kelliher and Sons, millers and general merchants of Tralee. She belonged to A Company Cumann na mBan. Her work was interrupted by the arrival of a messenger with orders from Madge Kidney, an officer of the company, instructing her to report immediately at the first aid centre at the Grand Hotel in Denny Street, where her comrades of Cumann na mBan were assembling. That was how she got the news of the landing and our advance on Tralee. The time was 'about eleven o'clock'. A fight was imminent, she was told, and the Republicans were mobilizing their available strength to oppose the Free Staters. Cumann na mBan was needed at the first-aid centre.

Without seeking the permission of her employers, Hanna
O'Connor left work and made haste to the Grand Hotel. She
remembered that the reception area and the dining-room were
already filling up with Cumann na mBan girls of all three
companies. Liz Anne O'Brien, leader of B Company, was in
charge. Among the other officers whom she saw in the hotel
were Madge Kidney and Mrs Pat Kennedy (Moyderwell), both
of A Company; Nora Hurley (later Mrs P. Scannell), D
Company, and Molly O'Brien (later Mrs Carmody). 'We had
good stocks of medical supplies,' Hanna O'Connor continued.
'Immediately after the outbreak of the Civil War we began
making field dressings and packing first-aid kits. All members
of our company had obtained strong canvas material from which
we made kit-bags. We were shown how to make field dressings
by Dr Maurice Quinlan of Tralee and Dr Roger O'Connor
of Listowel, and were given rolls of cotton wool, bandages,
cards of safety pins, scissors, cleaning lotions and disinfectants,
which we wrapped and packed into the kit-bags. A large surplus
of first-aid material had already been sent to Ballymullen
barracks.'

Cumann na mBan was prepared, and although the
organization in Tralee was totally anti-Treaty, the members
were ready to tend the casualties of both armies.

5

ACTION ON THE ROAD
TO TRALEE

Our leading units came under brisk fire as we approached Kilfenora and there also we suffered our first casualty. Private Patrick Quinn was shot dead. The firing came from an ancient earthen ring fort that commanded a stretch of the road. Tommy Sheehy, OC of the Fenit garrison, had rallied his men and put a small detail into hurriedly chosen positions in the fort. They were unable to hold these for more than a few minutes. Driven from the fort, they retreated north-west in the general direction of Barrow rather than east towards Tralee.

There was no easing of our rapid advance. Immediately ahead and to the left of the road was Sammy's Rock, a formidable limestone formation rising in a gradual ascent to more than a hundred feet and dominating the ground most of the way back to Fenit, a distance of about two miles. Here we encountered brief but stiff resistance, our advance hotly disputed by the main body of the Fenit unit, which had taken up positions on the rock. As we moved forward at the double, loosely strung out and making use of every bit of the sparse cover, we saw Republican reinforcements climbing the rock from the Tralee side. They were too late and too ill-prepared to be effective as a serious delaying force. Nevertheless, they courageously joined the fight as they climbed, firing on us from exposed positions as we worked our way round the rock, but their weapons were no match for our fire power and overwhelming numbers. At that juncture, our armoured car, the 'Ex-Mutineer', made its appearance and under cover of intense fire, detachments of our troops determinedly stormed the height and dislodged the Republicans. They left one dead. John Sullivan of Aughacasla, Castlegregory, of Tadhg Brosnan's 4th Battalion, Kerry No 1 Brigade, was killed as he climbed the rock. We took six prisoners, one of whom was wounded. Our casualties were Lieutenant Martin Nolan and some privates wounded. The engagement had been short, sharp and decisive.

There was no cover on the slopes and no way that Paddy Paul Fitzgerald and his section could have made it to the top. Moreover, we were already on their left flank in a manoeuvre to encircle the rock.

Michael McMahon, a Strand Road Company Lieutenant in the 9th Battalion, was with the section that had attempted to climb to positions on Sammy's Rock. On getting word that we had landed at Fenit, he immediately reported at his mobilization centre, which was the police barracks at High Street in Tralee, and joined the hastily assembled section of fourteen or sixteen men, mostly of his own company, that was rushed out to Oyster Hall in the lorry driven by Mick McGlynn. In his recollection of that morning, the section included Dan Jeffers, Tom Sharkey, Denis Keane, Jimmy Keane, David Barry, Jamsey Murphy, Pat McKenna, M. Whelan (Ardfert) and John Sullivan. There were others whose names he could not remember. 'Our transport dropped us at Oyster Hall,' he recalled. 'We heard heavy firing ahead and raced towards Sammy's Rock. At a bend in the road we were intercepted by Paddy Paul Fitzgerald and Paddy Garvey. They warned us that the Staters were just ahead. Paddy Paul led us in an attempt to climb the rock and link with Tommy Sheehy and his men who were on top and blazing away with their rifles. They could not have had much ammunition, but they were generously letting the Staters have what stuff they had.' Looking back over half a century and more, he readily conceded that Fitzgerald was in imminent danger of losing his small force. 'Some of Sheehy's men had been surrounded and captured,' he said, 'and he had lost Johnny Sullivan, killed half way up the bare slope. We were fortunate to extricate ourselves from an impossible situation and get back across the fields to Seafield House, Donovan's old place, where we took up fresh positions. We were joined there by more men from Tralee. I remember that John (Gal) Slattery was one of them.

We were too few and were quickly driven from these positions also. With Jeffers and McKenna, I withdrew to Ballyroe. We remained there that night, as the Staters had got between us and Tralee.'

Jim Higgins had been working in a field by the roadside under the shadow of Sammy's Rock and 'was legging it to the house' as fast as he could when he heard the Crossley with its load of Republicans pull up at Oyster Hall. 'They rushed over this way and started to climb the rock,' he recalled, 'and I saw the Staters open up on them with rifles and machine-guns and they were firing from an armoured car, too. The Republicans hadn't a chance. There was only a handful of them and they were lucky to get away with only one man dead. But the Staters were on their heels and a couple of them were captured over the road. My cousin Tom Flynn got as far as the Spa but he was killed there. One of the Staters was killed over near Kilfenora. He was shot through the throat. More of them were wounded here on the road. Over at the house I peeped through a window and watched the Staters going past. Some of the crayters were dead tired.'

Higgins laughed as he recalled 'a bunch of bank clerks from Tralee' who were camping at the foot of Sammy's Rock. 'When the lead started flying, I tell you they were not long clearing off without a bother about their things.'

Paddy Paul Fitzgerald was with some men of his battalion who had succeeded in getting away from the rock. He was anxious to get back to Tralee with them at once but found that Liston's car had been driven off and they were 'left stranded' on the road. 'We had no choice but to beat back towards town at the double,' he recalled. 'Our group became separated. Tom Flynn, the Fenit Company Adjutant, was with me and we got as far as the Spa. We entered Dan Lyons's pub and went out by the back door into the fields. The Staters were near, and I felt that our best chance of avoiding capture was to go over to Din Joe Nolan's house. Tom disagreed. He said we should go down to the beach, as we had a good chance of getting beyond the Spa Cross ahead of them by making a dash along the shore. I decided to go along with his advice. Down with us through the fields and we were running by the shore when fire was opened on us.'

From an upstairs room in the Healy home at the Spa, Tom Healy and his brother Joe, a medical student at the time, saw the troops break down a wooden door that gave entrance to Maurice O'Callaghan's garden (Kent Lodge) on the sea side of the road. Shortly afterwards they heard the sound of firing coming from the beach.

Paddy Paul Fitzgerald continued: 'Sections of the Staters had reached the Cross and others were behind us. We exchanged fire with them and Tom was killed beside me on the beach. I was rushed and captured. Back on the road I joined six of our men who were prisoners. We were marched off towards Tralee under close guard.' The war was over for all seven.

As Commandant of the 1st (Tralee) Battalion, John Joe Sheehy was also OC Ballymullen barracks. Although the landing at Fenit was not what he expected (he had thought Tarbert the most likely place), it was on his advice that the garrison was put into the coastguard station and the viaduct mined early in July. The mine layer was Jimmy Ryle from Farmer's Bridge, a Valentia-trained communications engineer who had worked for the P and O Line in the Orient. Early in the war also, Sheehy had selected defensive positions in Tralee town, chosen to deal with attack from the west or from the north side. By far the most formidable of these was Latchford's mill, an immensely strong structure rising four storeys over ground floor accommodation. From its site at the top of Nelson (now Ashe) Street, the top three storeys gave a field of fire down the New Line as far as Kelliher's mill and down Nelson Street towards Castle Street as far as St John's Church of Ireland Church; likewise it dominated the north side and east towards the entrance to the Great Southern and Western Railway station. Another post, behind a strong wall that enclosed the property of the railway company at the top of Edward Street, had a clear field of fire to the Tralee and Dingle Railway station and yard at the top of Nelson Street. Men placed there would support the positions in Latchford's mill and also engage troops attempting to force their way past the northern side of the mill to gain the Great Southern and Western marshalling yards and thence follow the railway line skirting Boherbee as a stage in an encircling operation. Positions covering the nearby North Kerry Railway tracks and gates were also chosen to oppose an encircling force. These three positions were ideally sited to deal with troops advancing over the New Line (as Commandant McGuinness, leading our main body, decided to do by way of a tactical diversion from the general plan) and to assist Vice-Commandant Dempsey's advance by the railway line.

The positions were not manned on D Day.

Immediately John Joe Sheehy learned of the landing, he collected a car, and with two armed men, one of whom was the driver, sped out towards Fenit on a fact-finding mission, his purpose being to observe the strength and movement of our troops. He was not aware that Mike McGlynn had been assigned a similar task by the acting Brigade Adjutant. Sheehy suspected sabotage and treachery at Fenit. How else could the Staters have got ashore? he asked himself. Near Oyster Hall, about half a mile on the Tralee side of Sammy's Rock, he came upon retreating Republicans who reported that they had been driven from the rock and that there was 'nothing left to oppose the Staters'. They told him that we were about five hundred strong, strung out in a long column with an armoured car in support, and were advancing rapidly along the coast road. He realized that we must reach Tralee within a couple of hours at the most.

The debacle at Fenit brought the moment of truth to John Joe Sheehy, whose battalion was responsible for the defence of Tralee. He had already suffered two heavy losses: One was that of Jerry Myles's column at Raheelty near Thurles in mid-July, which deprived him of many trained and battle-tested fighting men; the other was that of Tadhg Brosnan's column, then on war service somewhere in County Limerick. Even more serious for him was the dissension in the brigade which had resulted in the refusal of the Strand Road Company to serve as a unit of his battalion since April 1921. He knew well that the 9th Battalion, formed four days earlier as a compromise solution to the brigade problem, was not in a state of readiness to make an effective stand against our rapid advance from Fenit. Furthermore, the formation of the new battalion had officially and formally removed the Strand Road Company from his command. 'Thus it happened,' he recalled, 'that in the hour of crisis not many seasoned combat troops were immediately available for the defence of the town.' The training and instruction of a reserve had necessarily been restricted to basics because of the problem of withdrawing men from their work places when funds were not available to compensate them or their families for loss of earnings. Apart from the limitations imposed on him by the course of events, Sheehy had come to appreciate the futility of locking up troops in defensive positions in buildings that must be overrun and isolated if not taken by assault; he had learned the lesson of Dublin. He now decided that his immediate priority must be to burn Ballymullen barracks. The Free State Army must be denied its immense value as a secure base for a large force. This done, he and his available men would fight as best they could, using positions from which they could withdraw to fight again on a day of their choosing.

The burning of Ballymullen barracks had to be a hurried operation. Three sick Volunteers (Devane, Moriarty and Prenderville) were hastily evacuated. Then petrol was quickly and liberally sloshed over floors and furniture. Ropes drenched with petrol trailed out through windows.

'Minutes after I gave the signal to vacate the building,' John Joe Sheehy recalled, 'the ropes were ignited and with a roar a section of the barracks burst into flames. Then we almost had tragedy. Two of our men narrowly escaped with their lives. Unknown to me, they were still in a second-floor dormitory when the ropes were fired. Flames barred their way to the stairs. We had to smash window bars free of their sockets to get the men out by a window. Then they climbed down a ladder. It was a near thing and it cost us valuable time. Our car, a temperamental Model T Ford with a will of its own, having indicated that it was not in a mood for further duties, we doubled across the camp field at the rear of the barracks compound and raced down Boherbee.'

A lorry was parked near the Sportsfield (Austin Stack Park) in Boherbee, and Sheehy had it driven down to Moyderwell

Cross and drawn up broadside, so that it formed the basis of a barricade barring the way to Boherbee, Moyderwell and Ballymullen from Upper Castle Street. Sacks of flour and meal from shops owned by Con Flahive and Johnny Collins were piled about the lorry; Collins had been a prison warder and was known as 'Face the Wall' Collins.

Sheehy put two men, Tom Foley and Mossy Galvin, into the corner house at the Cross. From a window position in an upstairs room above the barricade they guarded the entrance to Moyderwell. The house, which belonged to James J. O'Hara, was demolished some years ago to make the Cross safer for traffic. O'Hara had a pawnshop on the ground floor. His son Tony was a pre-Truce member of A Company. Another son, Dermot, would become a brilliant pupil of Colonel Fritz Brase at the Army School of Music, from which he graduated with distinction and later achieved the prestigious position of leader of the No 1 Army Band.

Sheehy also placed men in O'Mahony's and Carrick's at the Cross and at the entrance to Boherbee. They took up window positions which were protected with bedding and anything else suitable that was near to hand. From these posts, the houses and the barricade, he was hopeful that the approach to Boherbee and Moyderwell from Castle Street could be kept under rifle fire and our advance held up as long as his ammunition lasted. Then he and his men would fade away to await another day. 'Our positions were vulnerable,' he recalled. 'We could be outflanked and encircled from the Town Park and the Great Southern railway tracks, and I was anxious on that account. There was also the formidable threat posed by the armoured car; I had only rifles.' To the best of his recollection, the men with him included Ned Looney, the tailor; Tom Connor, the barber; Tucker Mahony, an ex-British soldier who had come through the 1914-18 war without a scratch; Tommy Duggan and Paddy Comerford, two other ex-British soldiers. Comerford, who was a linotype operator at *The Kerryman*, had been a machine-gunner in France. Also with him were Paddy Moriarty, Dixon Fitzgerald, Michael Bower, 'Sidecar' Connor, Jack Dowling, Dick O'Sullivan, and Henry Carrick. Before the Staters came in sight, they were joined by Miko

Leary, OC Fianna Éireann (Tralee), Pat O'Donnell from Riverside, Tony Gorman of D Company Rock Strand and 'some other names I can't recall. Tony told us that the RIC barracks was in flames.'

When Johnny Connor of the Farmer's Bridge–Ballyseedy Company came down Boherbee carrying a Lewis gun, John Joe Sheehy was very glad to see him. 'Johnny was a fine officer and a thundering great fighter,' he recalled. 'We discussed how best we could make the Staters pay a price for the town, and agreed he would be of most value with the Lewis in the Rock Street or Strand Street sector.' Connor set off for the west end of the town and met Michael Fitzgerald, brother of Paddy Paul, at the 9th Battalion assembly centre. Together they went round to the back door of the Shamrock mills (Russell Arcade), then owned by Robert McCowen and Sons. Fitzgerald smashed the lock and led the way to the roof. Connor trained his Lewis gun on the spot where Pembroke Street makes a right-angle junction with Rock Street. Then they awaited events. They did not have long to wait.

About midday a number of Cumann na mBan girls were sent out from their first-aid centre in the Grand Hotel on a familiarization round of the Republican positions in the town. Hanna O'Connor went with Maimie McSweeney (Mrs. Pat Moriarty), also of A Company: 'Maimie and I covered the Rock, Pembroke Street and the New Line, where we came upon a group of Republicans in a shed. They told us that our men had taken over the Shamrock mills in Bridge Street. We went there and spoke to Johnny Connor of Farmer's Bridge, who was in charge. He had a machine-gun positioned on the roof of the building. Johnny and the men with him were in great heart, as indeed were all the men we met on our round of the positions.'

Their duty completed, the girls returned to their base at the Grand Hotel. 'By that time,' Hanna O'Connor added, 'Father Ayres OP and Dr Maurice Quinlan were with us. Soon afterwards heavy firing broke out at the western end of the town.'

6

THE HARD BATTLE
FOR TRALEE

Little more than an hour after the *Lady Wicklow* was brought to berth at Fenit, we had passed Sammy's Rock and were on the road to Tralee, five miles distant. On our right, the road was bounded by the sea and on our left by the Tralee and Fenit Railway tracks. There was a brief halt at the Spa, where the first part of the plan to encircle Tralee and close in on Ballymullen barracks was put into effect.

Captain Billy McClean and his column of Dublin Guards moved off from the Spa and proceeded along by the shore to enter Tralee at Caherina, three miles further on. In accordance with instructions, he was then to detach a force to encircle the town from the west side, by Blennerville, Ballyard, Ballymullen Castle and thence to Ballymullen barracks; in this part of the operation he had the fortunate assistance of a native of the area, Sergeant Jack Lydon. With the remainder of the column, McClean would continue his advance into the town by Strand Road and, in the vicinity of the Square and Bridge Street, make contact with the main force, due to enter at Pembroke Street.

At the junction of the Fenit road with the Ardfert–Tralee road, a second encircling force was detached under Vice-Commandant Jim Dempsey. He had orders to proceed by the railway line skirting the town as far as the workhouse on the eastern side, and from there to advance along Workhouse Road and down Ballymullen to the military barracks.

Both encirclement tasks were carried out with precision.

Our main body, under the immediate command of Jim McGuinness, with Sonny Conroy his second in command, turned towards Tralee, down past Mounthawk towards Pembroke Street, about a mile distant. We were still advancing rapidly but with caution now, and eventually we came under fire at Balloonagh as we approached the Tralee and Dingle Railway gates at the entrance to Pembroke Street. The gates (and the gates of Strand Road) ceased to exist with the closing of the Tralee and Dingle Railway in 1953. Today, a traffic crossing (Matt Talbot Road) separates Pembroke Street from Balloonagh at this point. The time was 1.30 p.m, three hours after the *Lady Wicklow* anchored at Fenit.

Jack Mason of A Company, 1st Battalion, was with a Republican unit charged with the task of locking the railway gates at Pembroke Street and further securing them with chains. This done, the unit had orders to link with sections that had taken up positions covering the gates with the object of containing the Free State advance as long as possible. The men in these sections belonged to different companies. Mason remembered that John O'Connor, Captain of D Company, was in charge of his unit. Members of his own company in Pembroke Street included Maurice (Moss) Maher, Tommy Vale, Bobby Barry and Paddy Barry. 'We stalled the Staters for a while,' he said, 'but had to withdraw when they closed in on us from several directions, having gained the railway tracks by crossing fields. Exposed to frontal and enfilading fire, we were quickly dislodged and had to clear out of our positions as fast as we could. Most of us retreated down Rock Street and joined others at the back of the police barracks or on the roof of Willie Horgan's, facing up Rock Street from both points. I was at the back of the barracks. Men of D Company went up Strand Road and entered Lunham's and Caherina House.'

Troops advancing to force the railway gates at Pembroke Street were under heavy fire from nearby Republican positions and from points in the Strand Road direction on our right. We had some wounded, but the troops smashed their way through the gates and the advance continued to the right-angle junction of Pembroke Street with Rock Street. Here death awaited six Dublin Guards and a medical orderly. Emerging into Rock Street, the troops were cut down by rifle and machine-gun fire, coming principally from the Shamrock mills and from other points not easily identified. These defence points caused not only dead and wounded casualties but also a serious hold-up of the advance into the town.

Back at the Pembroke Street railway gates part of the main force turned to the right and attempted an entry by the Strand Road railway gates, but they too came under heavy fire from posts at Lunham's and Caherina House. The Republicans in these houses included men who had withdrawn from the Spa and from Pembroke Street and its immediate vicinity. The attempt was not pressed.

'From our window position in Lunham's,' Jim O'Shea recalled, 'Jack McCarthy and I saw the Staters advance in extended formation along the railway line and we blazed away at them. We wounded several and later collected three or four of their rifles. They responded with rifle fire on Lunham's, and mortar round the window casement showered down on us and into our eyes. Men from other units joined us. They were detailed to take up positions in the top floor of the house. The Staters withdrew and took their wounded with them.'

Paddy Cahill, who had assumed command of the available 9th Battalion troops, entered Lunham's and congratulated the men posted there on their success in driving back the attackers. 'He then ordered us to move up to Caherina House,' O'Shea said, 'as Lunham's was known to the Staters and they were bound to come back. We saw smoke rising from the RIC barracks. It was set on fire by a section of the Strand Road Company.'

At Rock Street, where Free State casualties were growing to serious proportions, Brigadier O'Daly seized a Red Cross flag and waved it frantically to indicate that medical stretcher bearers were about to go to fallen soldiers in the street. Private Patrick Harding of the Medical Corps, along with a companion soldier, rushed to aid a stricken comrade. As he bent to lift the casualty on to a stretcher he was shot to death and fell across the soldier he was attempting to lift. His companion was also hit and wounded.

The battle continued to rage and O'Daly finally determined

that the Republican positions must be eliminated. He called upon Captain Charlie Downey (lately of the Dublin Active Service Unit) to charge them. Dave Neligan recalled how, standing beside O'Daly, he saw Downey 'visibly pale' at the order, but, like the fine soldier that he was, he assembled some equally brave soldiers to go with him. Under cover fire provided by the afterwards notable 'Jock, the machine-gunner', Sergeant Dan Mullen, standing fearlessly in the centre of Rock Street and with his powerful strength firing a Lewis gun from his shoulder, the soldiers charged the point of greatest danger.

The defenders withdrew and succeeded in avoiding capture by McClean's detachment moving at their rear by Strand Road. Johnny Connor and Michael Fitzgerald got into Johnny O'Donnell's shop in Bridge Street (now John Dowling's) and, slipping out through a back yard gate, managed to reach the Dingle Railway tracks. Jack Mason and some others 'holed up' in the Jeffers Institute at 1 Day Place, across the street from where they had been posted in the yard of the former RIC barracks. 'Jack Dee's wife worked next door and she brought us food,' he recalled, 'and when darkness came down we got out by a window at the rear of the house and moved back to Derrymore. Jack Dee was a member of A Company.'

The firing from the Strand Road direction ceased on the appearance of additional Free State troops and the arrival of the armoured car in the town. Jim O'Shea and his comrades remained quietly in Caherina House until after nightfall, 'to our surprise, our presence there apparently not known to the Staters'. They moved out in darkness and went up to Ballyard before turning west towards Derryquay. 'We met Father Ayres the Dominican at Healy's Cross,' O'Shea recalled, 'and he asked if anybody wanted confession. We all did. He asked us to remove our caps and gave us general absolution. Jack McCarthy and I stayed at Savage's Lodge in Annagh, and the rest of the lads went back to Derryquay School.'

The way was now clear at Rock Street for the Dublin Guards to gather their dead and wounded and prepare to resume the advance, via Bridge Street, to the Mall, where they were due to link with Captain McClean's main party entering the town on their right via Strand Road, Bridge Street or the Square, to the Mall. The dead were removed to O'Keeffe's Stores in Rock Street, which was used as a temporary mortuary.

The engagement at Rock Street had caused a build-up of troops extending back towards the railway gates at Pembroke Street. At that point, and in the midst of the battle, I approached Commandant McGuinness and told him I could bring him by a different route into the centre of the town. He told me to lead the way. I brought him around the New Line to the top of Nelson Street, where the Tralee and Dingle Railway station stood. At that point of entry to the town, Latchford's mill dominated the surrounding roads, as it does to this day. John Joe Sheehy had prepared strong defensive positions at the mill for just such an eventuality as was now taking place. Fortunately for me as a guide and therefore front runner, this particular defence point was not manned. It could have proved more devastating than those at Rock Street.

With Commandant McGuinness and his strong detachment of troops I moved into Nelson Street. After more than half a century of time I can still recall the kaleidoscope of thought as I advanced with the first soldiers of the new state into a street so specially familiar to me since boyhood. This was the street where I played with my school friends Percy Hanafin and Jerry Myles. Now there were no familiar faces to be seen; no faces of any kind in fact! The Tralee people were indoors, some perhaps peering through drawn curtains or raised window blinds. On we went, spread out in single file on both sides of the street to minimize the effect of any sudden burst of gun-fire; on past St John's Church of Ireland Church, where I had watched the red-coated soldiers of another time march with their bands to divine service and stack their arms outside; on past the Protestant Hall — how identifiable the names were in those days — now private law offices. Opposite was the imposing Tralee courthouse, scene of famous Land League trials, with its massive steps and protective cannons, reminders of colonial conquests and wars of long ago. How often as a boy had I watched with awe the mounted RIC, with their funny little round hats, escort the ermine and scarlet-robed Assize Judges as they arrived and departed in their horse-drawn carriages with all the attendant pomp and ceremony of their imperial role. Then on a little further in this so familiar street, past the house where, in 1877, my father, the first President of the Tralee Branch of the Land League, had founded the Land League newspaper, *The Kerry Sentinel.*

But thoughts like these had to be brushed aside in the harsh realities of gunfire and death. By our movement through Nelson Street to its juncture with Lower Castle Street we had outflanked the Republican positions at the Shamrock mills and the RIC barracks. It was a grim moment. Not surprisingly these streets were also deserted by the people; as elsewhere in the town they remained indoors. It was for us now to probe and find out where the next defences were located. That did not take very long. We moved around, but there seemed to be no opposition except from a small post at Harty's, which was quickly silenced. We found the first–aid centre set up by Cumann na mBan at the Grand Hotel in Denny Street.

We turned to advance up Castle Street in the direction of Boherbee. I was with a companion soldier on the footpath on the right-hand side facing towards Boherbee. Suddenly I realized that the slight bend in the street made us more exposed to fire on that side if it should come from the direction of Moyderwell Cross, where, in fact, a strong defensive barricade had been erected. My companion was Private Tom Larkin, a fine-looking young soldier. I told him to move quickly to the far side with me. Even as I spoke and stepped off the footpath just outside the Bank of Ireland, I heard a sudden burst of gunfire. Instantly I turned, and saw my companion falling forward on the roadway, blood pouring from the roof of his head. As I ran to join our troops under cover on the opposite side of the street, I realized that I had had a miraculous escape. At once, Jim McGuinness, the man whose forceful leadership had been the drive behind the fast advance on Tralee, called on us to go and get Larkin. With three other soldiers, whom I did not know, I dashed back and helped to lift and carry him to the first aid-post in Denny Street. It was clear to me that he was seriously injured. I took his rifle, sticky with his blood, and ran to rejoin the advance along Castle Street towards Moyderwell Cross.

Heavy fire was coming from the barricade and nearby houses overlooking Castle Street. The troops were forced to seek shelter in doorways and shopfronts while gradually edging forward under covering fire. McGuinness detached a small section to seize the post-office in Edward Street, which was more or less on the route of advance. It had been occupied by the Republicans but they had withdrawn their men from it that day. Quick dashes enabled soldiers to gain the protective cover afforded by the wide Green Lane entrance to the Presentation Convent schools, quite close to the barricade and houses where the Republicans held positions. Soon a sizeable force had assembled in the lane. There was a long hold up there, about an hour, until the 'Ex-Mutineer' arrived with O'Daly, its business finished at the western end of the town. Once again, the armoured car proved to be the dominant factor in this kind of fighting. It poured its gunfire into the barricade and corner house positions, which were then charged by a party under Sonny Conroy. The defenders retreated by various escape routes, but some were captured.

John Joe Sheehy recalled that when the assault on his Moyderwell Cross positions was renewed, he and the men with him were dislodged from the barricade by rifle grenades. He was hit in the left arm by splinters and Ned Rooney received a thigh wound. 'We withdrew to the corner of a nearby house,' he continued. 'The armoured car drove up to the barricade but failed to force its way through. The crew remained inside and raked O'Hara's house with machine-gun fire to such purpose that I was certain the riflemen upstairs had been cut to pieces. Eventually the car was backed down and during a lull in the firing I was able to send Tom Connor to report on the situation in O'Hara's. To my relief, he found that our men had broken an opening into Tom Crimmins's house next door, from which they were able to get away unscathed. Some of us then got into the fields from Carrick's house and thus avoided being overrun when the Staters resumed the attack. We were hopelessly outnumbered and outgunned.'

Henry Carrick remembered that when the positions at Moyderwell Cross were no longer tenable, 'most of the men retreated into the Brewery gardens through the Casey, Skinner, Murphy, and Tom Fitzgerald (Lough) houses and Whetson's butcher shop.' From the back of the gardens they crossed the Tralee–Killarney railway line, pushed on through the old golf course by Racecourse Road and out towards Ballymacelligott. Carrick got away with a group that went from his house into the Mercy Convent grounds and Dean's Lane and then across the Damp field to the Ballymacelligott side. With him were 'Sidecar' Connor, Edward (Nedeen) Bower, Richard (Dixon) Fitzgerald, Paddy Comerford, Eugie Hogan and Paddy Moriarty.

Tony Gorman retreated by Dispensary Lane. 'Miko Leary, Bob Sugrue of Pembroke Street and Mick Foley from Blennerville were with me,' he recalled. 'From there we went up to the Great Southern Railway and dumped our rifles. We debated what to do next and decided to stay the night in a railway dormitory to avoid being caught by enemy patrols. It was not a good idea. They found us there early next morning and marched us off to the jail.'

Two Free State casualties were brought to the Cumann na mBan first-aid centre in the Grand Hotel. One died almost immediately. 'His name was Tommy Larkin,' Hanna O'Connor remembered. 'Father Ayres was asked to send his personal belongings to his next of kin as soon as they had been notified of his death.'

Fighting in the Moyderwell sector was still in progress when members of Cumann na mBan were sent out to look for casualties. 'With three other girls I went along the route taken by the Free State soldiers who had entered the town at Pembroke Street,' Hanna O'Connor continued, 'but we found no casualties, although we entered fields and looked behind hedges all the way to Clogherbrien Cross, about a mile from Pembroke Street railway gates. Apparently the casualties had been taken care of by the Free State medicals. It was about six o'clock when we got back to the hotel. We were then allowed home as we had had nothing to eat since morning.'

The Dublin Guards moved rapidly forward, some straight ahead through Boherbee to take the staff barracks, others turning sharply to the right along by Moyderwell and Clonmore Terrace to Ballymullen barracks. I was with the latter party and we arrived to see flames and smoke coming from a right-hand corner section of the barracks. This was a detached building known as 'the Colonel's House' and used as an officers' Mess. It was the only part of the barracks that was burning badly, as far as I could see, although another section near the centre clock was also on fire. With a few others I went for a closer look at the detached building. That it was the officers' Mess was beyond doubt. We looked through the ground floor windows and could see a large table beautifully laid out with cold meats, bread and butter and milk. The sight was too much for our empty stomachs, and in seconds we were inside devouring what we could while watching the progress of the flames, now reaching the doorway to the Mess.

The flames grew more menacing and the ceiling began to indicate its intention of ending everything, but it gallantly held back while we feasted. Then we left as we had entered, through the ground floor windows, but perhaps a bit more quickly — and just in time.

It was 6.30 o'clock in the evening. The battle for Tralee was over, the mission accomplished, but the war in Kerry was only beginning.

7

AFTERMATH

In the evening summer sun I could afford to sit on the grass and relax while I watched the movement of troops arriving in Ballymullen barracks. They were coming in from different parts, their allotted tasks completed. Inevitably, confusion of a kind reigned, but out of it was emerging the discipline and organization which had maintained the force throughout its fine operation. I had no special unit assignment and, therefore, no bothersome officers, non-commissioned or otherwise, to chivvy me around. In my newly acquired job as guide I was, because of my local knowledge, called on later to bring officers to the sources in the town where they could attend to such matters as food supplies and printing, and coffins for the dead. It was a situation of personal freedom which continued quite happily for me, even for some time after I received my officer rank a few weeks later.

Ballymullen barracks had an extensive area for reassembly. Looking around, I could see that rather more damage than I had at first thought had been done to the front portion of the main block. It was more than half a century later that I learned from the officer who had command of the 1st (Tralee) Battalion, John Joe Sheehy, that he had personally directed the burning before setting up the barricade which had impeded our advance at Moyderwell Cross. However, the greater portion of the barracks remained intact, including billeting, cooking, dining and administrative quarters. No doubt this could be attributed to the speed of the encircling movement which held the threat of capture for Sheehy and the men he had with him to carry out the burning.

I saw the armoured car arrive in barracks. It had given extensive and menacing support to the troops in all parts since the landing at Fenit eight hours earlier. Later came the 18-pounder field piece, drawn on its own wheels by Egan's horse. Dave Neligan proffered Mossy Egan three pound notes, which was money in those days. The young farmer looked at him. 'Is that not enough?' Neligan asked. ''Tis indeed, Sir,' Egan replied, 'and I think I'd like to join ye altogether now.' So he did, in fact, and later served with the rank of sergeant under Commandant Sean Hayes in the Army (Special Unit) at GHQ. The field piece, named 'The Rose of Tralee' by the troops, was in action on only two occasions in Kerry, so far as I can recall, the first during the advance on Castleisland a few days after the capture of Tralee. It was brought into action again at the Droum ambush later in the month, an hour-long battle near the Pap mountains beyond Killarney, when Jim McGuinness sustained a head wound and was temporarily a prisoner of the Republicans.

Outposts were established in the town to ensure that the ground captured would not be retaken. Those immediately set up were: The Jeffers Institute, Day Place (now Touche Ross); O'Leary's, the Mall (Town and Country Pub); the upper part of Baily's, the Mall/Ashe Street (FAS-Manpower office); Tylers, Bridge Street; William Horgan's and O'Connor & Prenderville's, Rock Street (Brogue Inn); Co-operative Wholesale Society's premises, Rock Street (business center); Jeremiah O'Keeffe's Stores, Pembroke Street (snooker hall); Slattery's Stores, Rock Street (Flynn's Stores); Watson's, 'Fortlands', Ballyard (Dowling's); Post-Office, Edward Street; staff barracks, Boherbee (St Patrick's Community Center and houses); the workhouse, Mileheight (Kerry County Council headquarters). Army headquarters was at Ballymullen barracks. The workhouse was very soon afterwards named Brian Houlihan barracks in honour of Captain Brian Houlihan of Kenmare, a Dublin Guards officer and 1916 veteran, who was killed in action near Castleisland a few days after the landing at Fenit.

The town firmly in our hands, no time was lost before patrols were active on round-up and search duties. Some forty prisoners captured during the fighting or later on during the evening included a former senior brigade officer, William (Billy)

Mullins, who had been Quartermaster on the staff displaced with Paddy Cahill (to whom he remained totally loyal) at the reorganization of the IRA in Kerry during the spring and summer of 1921. After Cahill, he was closest to Austin Stack during the preparations to receive the German arms shipment expected on Easter Sunday 1916. In the War of Independence he fought in the Kerry No 1 Brigade active service unit that was formed and led by Cahill. Mullins kept two hackney cars and was in Cahirciveen with a fare when news of our landing at Fenit reached Tralee. All was quiet in the town by the time he got back to his home in Moyderwell that night. He remained a prisoner for the duration of the Civil War.

The prisoners were placed under the control of Captain Jack Harpur in the jail, a short distance from the military barracks. The rounding-up process was largely assisted by Eamon Horan and some of his followers who had come to join the forces in the barracks. In fact, I travelled in the armoured car with him on a search of the Ballyard area on the night of the landing. He and his friends could more easily identify known Republican troops who had not linked up with their comrades who were now retreating and re-grouping in outlying areas such as Farmer's Bridge, Ballymacelligott, Farranfore, Currans, Firies and Castleisland, as well as in 9th Battalion area, including Barrow, Churchill, Curraheen and Derrymore.

So in the evening of that August day the spectacular mission of the Dublin Guards had been accomplished; an expedition undertaken and executed with skill, courage and drive, and planned and directed by officers whose only training in military tactics and administration was what they had acquired in the course of lectures and demonstrations in their own IRA training camps. Perhaps the most striking feature of the action that I recall was its momentum after the landing. The pier was rushed so as to capture Fenit village and prevent explosives being used to destroy the pier itself, the coastguard building and the former RIC barracks. This was the first essential. From then on it was unrelenting forward movement. There was no delay, there were no rests, with stoppages only at fight points — Kilfenora, Sammy's Rock, the Spa, Pembroke Street–Rock Street, Strand Street, Castle Street and Boherbee–Moyderwell.

The movement was always forward until the final target of Ballymullen barracks was reached, nine miles and eight hours after the landing, on foot with heavy equipment and after thirty-six hours at sea. They were indeed fine soldiers, well officered.

A dispatch from Paddy Cahill, in command of a 9th Battalion column, speaks with fair appreciation of the situation on the day following the capture of Tralee. It was intended for Humphrey Murphy, OC Kerry No 1 Brigade, who had moved his headquarters to a point in the parish of Currans, about eight miles south-east of Tralee, Cahill had his own head-quarters at Curraheen, a small townland situated some five miles west of Tralee and about halfway between the town and Camp on the coastal road to Dingle. The dispatch, which does not include a reference to the Rock Street battle, of which Johnny Connor had given him a verbal report, is as follows:

Curraheen
Thursday

A Cara,

I asked Johnny O'Connor of Farmer's Bridge to acquaint you of our whereabouts. He has possibly seen you today, and given you particulars of the landing, and seizure of Tralee by the Free Staters, and an account of the fighting. I tried to keep in touch with your acting OC, Jerh O'Leary, and John J. S[heehy] and as they advised us to retreat we did so as you know per Johnny. I do not know how many men Jerh O'L[eary] and John J. had with them but I am certain that they were very few, and last evening they were pretty well surrounded, but it is possible that they got through at night. I know that early in the day they held a position at O'Hara's, Moyderwell, and seem to have done fairly effective work as the Free Staters had a good many casualties around Denny Street and the Bank of Ireland. Another small post of ours was operating at Harty's (Mall), and did good work. Possibly these were a few of Mick Leary's scouts. The Fianna and Cumann na mBan were of the greatest assistance to us, particularly the latter as they were moving in the thick of the fight.

The total casualties on our side are two dead, Tom Flynn, Coy. Adjt., Fenit, shot dead at Oysterhall, and John Sullivan of Castlegregory, formerly Lieut. of D Coy., shot at the Spa, and as far as I know none wounded, except for one of the Fianna at Bridge Street, slightly in the leg. It is difficult to estimate the enemy's losses owing to the different rumours, but I consider 12 (twelve) killed and between 30 and 40 wounded should not be much wide of the mark.

I do not know the number captured with Paddy Paul [Fitzgerald] and P. Garvey, but Jeffers, P. McKenna, McMahon and about four or five more of B Coy. got away. Two Free Staters rifles were captured with 400 rounds .303 in Strand Street, and I understand C N mBan got two rifles and about 500 rounds of stuff in Rock Street area.

I am sending over P. Daly [Nap] to you tomorrow for instructions. I am bringing our chaps to Castlegregory tomorrow for Johnny Sullivan's funeral, and he (Daly) will report on number of rifles available to us. I should say about twenty when Jeffers and the others join us.

John L. [Sullivan] brought 13 men from Castlegregory, and 7 from Dingle with arms, including the Battn. officers to here last evening, but as I expected you would not attack Tralee without extra good reinforcements I suggested that they return.

Dingle Barracks and Coastguard Station were burned by Battn. officers leaving yesterday, and their Hqrs is now the Railway Station. We are in touch with Castle[gregory] and Dingle from here. We have one Crossley and four motors, but little petrol.

Enemy strength in Tralee about 500, between Fenit and Tralee 100 more — in Tralee, one armoured car whippet type and one small field piece; the party in charge of Brig. Daly. Enemy hold positions in Tralee—Workhouse, Ballymullen, Latchfords, Staff Barracks, Watsons (Ballyard), Jeffers Institute, Foresters Hall, Tylers, Galvins, Republican Hqrs, and O'Keeffe's, Pembroke Street.

More reinforcements expected at Fenit. I do not think it likely. Tarbert is more probable for drive on Listowel, and then link up with Limerick.

Horan, Lydon, Hoare and O'Hara (of Tralee) were with Free Staters from Fenit and I understand a number are joining from Tralee.

Mise,

P.S. O'C.

P.S. M. O'Leary (Fianna) is still in Tralee and all right. Bombs were thrown last night, with what effect I do not know.

Most notable is the indication that Cahill, the former brigadier, was co-operating with his replacement, Humphrey Murphy, Nevertheless, the divisive element, which over a period of more than fifteen months had seriously reduced the efficiency of the brigade in Tralee town and district, would persist in the personal relationships; rank-and-file bitterness between men who gave their loyalty to Paddy Cahill and those who accepted the authority and leadership of Humphrey Murphy would last a long time.

There are some inaccuracies in the report: John Sullivan was killed at Sammy's Rock and Tom Flynn at the Spa, and it was in Tralee that we were joined by Eamon Horan and his friends. Jack Lydon had, of course, accompanied us from Dublin. The reference to the Castleisland Battalion Commandant, Jerh O'Leary, as acting Brigade OC and being with John Joe Sheehy in Tralee on 2 August is puzzling. I could find no evidence to show that he had participated in the battle for the town. Moreover, the Brigade OC, Humphrey Murphy, was less than a dozen miles away, in his native Ballybeg.

Although we had no knowledge of the strength or disposition of the Republican forces at the time of our advance on Tralee, it was, as proved, a reasonable assumption that their withdrawing troops would for the most part make their way east towards Ballymacelligott and Castleisland, and west towards Curraheen and Derrymore. Hence the purpose of the detachments under Jim Dempsey and Billy McClean in the plan for encirclements of the town.

It is strange to find that an officer of Mick McGlynn's competence and courage had no part in the fighting. In his own words: 'I was sent to the Mileheight, a mile or so from the town on the way to Killarney or Castleisland, and my orders were to intercept any of our forces returning from the defensive positions they had held in the counties of Limerick and Tipperary, and also to establish a rallying point for those leaving Tralee. Eddie McCarthy and John Byrne, the creamery manager from Ballymac[elligott], helped me to set up an attack unit covering the main road out of Tralee. It was getting dusk when we abandoned the position. I spent the night at Farmer's Bridge with Johnny Connor and Mossy Galvin. Next day I moved to Castleisland and joined in a reorganization of our forces.'

The late evening and night of 2 August were relatively quiet in Tralee. Sporadic firing and explosions took place, but this was to be expected after a day of combat. An occasional sentry observing too intently the surrounding darkness of a new outpost can readily believe that enemies abound. Little doubt, too, that an occasional departing Republican found release in expressing his resentment by bomb or gunfire. Many waited in hiding until nightfall to make their getaway. Departing members of D (Rock Street) Company headed north towards Ballyroe.

News of the landing was late in reaching Batt Dowling, Captain of the Ballyroe Company, and with the news he also received orders to block roads and demolish bridges. With John McDonnell, Tommy Barton, Willie O'Neill and some others he blew up the river bridge at the Kerries to prevent an approach to Tralee by secondary road from the west at that point. They dealt similarly with the bridge near the strand on the way from the Spa towards the White Wall and Blennerville. Neither of these actions interfered with our advance.

Batt Dowling remembered that the mines used for the demolitions were made in Ballymullen barracks by Jimmy Daly of Killarney, a fitter employed by the Tralee and Dingle Railway Company. 'The Staters were entering the town by the time the mines were delivered to the Ballyroe Company,' he said, 'entirely too late for us to make effective use of them that day, and a pointer to the fact that the landing at Fenit had taken everybody by surprise. We did use some of the mines on subsequent days to blow up a section of the Fenit railway line, the railway bridge on the North Kerry line at Tubrid, and the bridge near Callaghan's of Ballyroe.'

Dowling ruefully recalled that he was surprised and captured in his own home by Free State troops on a night towards the end of August: 'Many local lads had joined the Staters and with their knowledge of the place and the likely movements of men on the run in the neighbourhood, it was difficult to escape the net. The same night, Hugh and Christy Ryan and Denis (Rory) O'Connor of D Company, together with Tommy Barton of my own company, were caught in Callaghan's of Ballyroe Hill. Joe Barrett of D Company and Henry Carrick of A Company were captured in Doon, a couple of miles from the town.'

The mines not used by the Ballyroe Company were dumped. Many years later they were found in the back garden of a house in Oakpark and destroyed by the military. Jimmy Daly, who made the mines, had a rifle and ammunition in his possession when captured by Free State troops and he was executed by firing-squad in Ballymullen barracks on 20 January 1923, along with John Clifford of Caherciveen, Michael Brosnan of Ballymacelligott and James Hannon of Causeway. They had been given the death sentence by a secret military court set up under the Army Emergency Powers Act.

When Hanna O'Connor of Cumann na mBan arrived, tired and hungry, at her home at Murphy's Terrace in Ballymullen after the battle for Tralee had ended, Dr Quinlan was there, talking to her father, Terence O'Connor. They were discussing the situation of the three Republican soldiers, Tim Devane, Moriarty and Jack Prenderville, who had been under doctor's care in the military barracks and were hurriedly evacuated before John Joe Sheehy set fire to the buildings. The three were now in a friendly house in Ballymullen, in a room over a bar and grocery shop, but there were fears that daily visits by a doctor would be noticed and give rise to suspicion that would lead to their capture. While Hanna was having a meal,

Dr Quinlan and her father decided that the men should be moved elsewhere. The doctor would take Devane and Moriarty in his car to his home in Ballyard and Prenderville would remain overnight in Ballymullen.

'The transfer of Devane and Moriarty to Ballyard was made quickly and uneventfully,' Hanna O'Connor remembered, 'and Dr Quinlan returned to our house. He had brought first-aid kits and blankets, maps and books from the Grand Hotel to the house after firing ceased and he now asked me to help him get them to the Republican troops outside the town. The items had been packed in large canvas bags which we loaded into his car and we then headed for Timothy Galvin's farmhouse a couple of miles south of Tralee.'

The question of moving Jack Prenderville was raised in Galvin's. 'He was well known to the family,' Hanna O'Connor continued, 'and they hit upon a simple plan to get him out of the danger zone. Mick Galvin, one of the boys who took the milk from the farm to Watson's creamery (later the Lee Strand) by pony and cart, would call at the shop to buy groceries on his way home by Ballymullen. Prenderville, who would be awaiting his arrival, would slip out of the house and sit in the cart, taking the reins as the driver. Mick Galvin would sit beside him, and hopefully they would drive to safety. The plan worked to perfection next day, even though they were held up and searched in upper Ballymullen. A soldier examined the milk churns and, finding them empty, waved on the driver. In a short time the third man was safe in the Galvin home.'

The very few writers who have attempted an account of the Civil War tend to treat the capture of Tralee as a military brush-aside, accomplished by Free State forces with little opposition. They point to the absence of the best units of the Kerry No 1 Brigade in the Limerick–Tipperary–Waterford area. While it is true that the columns sent from Kerry to hold sectors of the Limerick–Waterford 'line' were made up to a large extent of trained and experienced fighting men, thereby causing a serious defence loss in the Tralee district, it is also true that sufficient combat troops remained to defend the area had the brigade staff been alert to the probability of a landing at Fenit. If proof is needed to refute the idea of an easy passage for the Free State troops one has only to remember that nine soldiers of the Dublin Guards died in the operation and that an unascertained number, possibly as many as thirty-five, were wounded. There is no existing record of the actual number wounded.

It has been said to me, in conversation with some surviving Republican officers in Tralee, that only a small 'maintenance party' remained to offer defence against the landing. This, as an excuse, I find unacceptable. They were the victims of surprise in the sixth week of the war. A fateful slackness in the brigade allowed us to catch the Fenit garrison totally off guard, and, on the following morning, permitted Colonel-Commandant Michael Hogan and his 240 troops to land unopposed at Tarbert.

The alert from Fenit gave, at the most, about three hours' notice to the Republicans in Tralee. It is to the credit of those who responded so quickly to the alarm and occupied hastily chosen positions that they fought with courage against what must have seemed to them a formidable array of Free State troops.

As might be expected, the landing forces suffered the greater casualties. The defenders occupied positions with selected fields of fire and even though these were not as fully manned as they could have been, nevertheless the troops were on familiar ground and for that reason were positioned where they could cause most damage. This was particularly so at Rock Street and Strand Street, where we of the advancing Dublin Guards sustained our greatest number of casualties. It was fortunate for us that other defence points, especially that at Latchford's mill, were not occupied.

The Republicans suffered relatively minor casualties; two killed and a few wounded; there is no recorded list. Again, the nature of the defence right through, being of a limited holding and sharp withdrawal character, favoured the infliction of casualties without serious risk of quick retaliation or capture. In this kind of defence, however, there was no possibility of stemming the advance and preventing the capture of Tralee.

The high proportion of Dublin Guards killed in relation

to the number wounded was, no doubt, due to the troops coming under immediate and devastating fire in exposed positions and from unexpected quarters, which could not be quickly identified and silenced. Those killed (all of Dublin city unless otherwise stated) were: Sergeant Fred Gillespie (age 23), B Company, 2nd Battalion, 11 Kenmare Parade, North Circular Road; Corporal Michael Farrell (27), machine-gunner, 2nd Eastern Division, 6 East James's Street; Corporal W. D. Carson (19), No 4 Company, 3rd Battalion, 122 University Avenue, Belfast; Private John Kenny (19), 16 Coombe Street; Private Thomas Larkin (27), A Company, 2nd Battalion, 'Shielmartin', Baily, Howth, County Dublin; Private James O'Connor (17), B Company, 73 Summerhill; Private Patrick Reilly (22), No 2 Company, 107 Lower Gardiner Street; Private Patrick Harding (19), Army Medical Service, 14 East James's Street, and Private Patrick Quinn (23), 18 Poolbeg Street.

I gleaned these particulars from the newspapers of the period and I was further helped in my inquiries by the courteous secretarial staff of Dublin Cemeteries at Glasnevin. The Department of Defence (Civil Service) was considerably less helpful and it was only after six months of persistent inquiry that I finally received some restricted information. Even this was inaccurate in stating the date of death as 3 August, the date inscribed on the memorial tablet at Glasnevin. The correct date should read 2 August 1922.

The *Lady Wicklow* took home the bodies of the Dublin Guards killed in the action. As an honour guard stood to attention, the nine coffins were placed side by side on a large dray owned by Con O'Leary, a railway carrier in Tralee, and conveyed to the Great Southern and Western Railway station, where they were put on rail for Fenit pier. The bodies were accompanied to Fenit by Guards officers and the honour guard. The *Lady Wicklow* arrived in Dublin in the afternoon of Saturday, 5 August, and the remains were at once conveyed to Portobello barracks. Michael Collins, Commander-in-Chief of the Free State Army, Richard Mulcahy, Chief of the General Staff, and Gearoid O'Sullivan, Adjutant-General, were amongst the officers present when the coffins were removed to the mortuary in the barracks.

On Tuesday, 8 August, six days after the Fenit landing, the bodies of the nine soldiers were buried in the Soldiers' Plot in Glasnevin cemetery, with full military honours, after a public funeral through the streets of Dublin.

Another member of the Dublin Guards was killed shortly after the capture of Tralee. When leaving the Spa on the journey into Tralee, Paddy O'Daly set up a post at Dan Lyons's pub and put in ten or twelve men to hold it. The post was attacked by the Republicans some days later and in this action Jack Lydon was killed. According to local sources, the attacking party included Jim Walsh of Churchill (a victim of the Ballyseedy mine in March 1923); Joe Sugrue and Christy Ryan, both of Tralee, and George Nagle of Ballygamboon, Castlemaine (killed at Derrynafeana, Killorglin, in April 1923) — three who belonged to D Company, 1st Battalion.

The story of the Fenit landing as told in these pages is the first factual account of that important episode of the Civil War. It was written long after the event itself took place, with the generous co-operation of survivors from both armies and of civilian eye witnesses; for this reason alone it is worth recording. Because of its nature, it relates more to the particular events in which the survivors had participated. It is hoped that the telling of the story now, even at this late stage, will clear the air and dispose of some of the inaccurate accounts published at one time or another. For example, there is the book on the Civil War which has a passage describing 'one notable incident' before the final capture of Tralee. 'This,' according to the author, 'was a miniature "armoured battle" which took place in the Moyderwell suburb between two anti-Treaty and two pro-Treaty armoured cars. For more than an hour these four-wheeled ironclads manoeuvred around each other, firing as they did so, through the streets of Tralee on the dull, wet and windy night that was August 2, 1922.'

There is no truth in this story. The only armoured car in Tralee was the 'Ex-Mutineer', which was brought to Fenit with the Dublin Guards aboard the *Lady Wicklow*. On the night in question, I travelled in that car with Eamon Horan in a search of Ballyard and other areas on the outskirts of

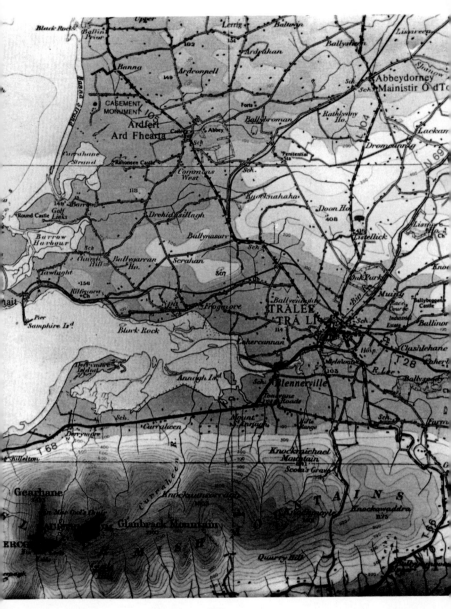

13 Map of Kerry

14 *Ceremonial occasion at Tralee Courthouse in the days of the British Empire*

15 *Denny Street, Tralee*

16 *Nelson (now Ashe) Street, Tralee*

17 *Ballymullen barrcks, Tralee*

18 Map of Tralee

n the 1898 Ordnance Survey map

19 *Michael Collins and Richard Mulcahy at the funeral of Arthur Griffith, in August 1922*

20 *The Regiment of Pearse, led by the author, in 1934*

21 *The unveiling of the memorial to Collins and Griffith by*
   W. T. Cosgrave on Leinster Lawn

22 *A group of IRA survivors at the unveiling of the Sonny McCarthy monument. In front: Jerry (Unkey) O'Connor. Front row: Tommy Sheehy, John Brassil, Jackie Price, Tommy (Nigger) Hussey, Jimmy (Nuts) O'Connor, Paddy Cantillon, Tom Sharkey. Back row: Tim Leahy, Michael Sullivan, Michael (Forker) McMahon, Joe Sugrue, Jimmy Shea, Pat (Nap) Daly*

7 Corrig House,
Corrig Avenue,
Dun Laoghaire,
Co. Dublin.

4th March 1977.

Dear Con,

We last met in a train heading for Dublin, you to Mountjoy Gaol after reprieve from sentence of death in Tralee, I to a posting out of Kerry after I had given evidence against the G.O.C. and others in connection with the Kenmare affair.

My recollection of our rather brief conversation concerned the Fenit landing on 2nd August 1922. You mentioned that the landing was opposed by a force of only six men and they had given a good account of themselves.

I wonder would you expand on that and on the subsequent events of that day only, 2nd August, in Tralee?

I have been trying to undertake a little research and find it difficult to get precise information about that particular day – NOT the period afterwards.

I am aware of a despatch from Curraheen concerning the landing and signed "P.S. O'C". Who was "P.S. O'C"? The report, understandably, is not too accurate.

23 *Letter from Niall Harrington to Con Casey*

he town. It was a fine night and we were not fired upon.

Another writer in *The Fenian*, an anti-Treaty mimeographed sheet published in Dublin, would have us know that 'British warships shelled Lackan coastguard station in the Kenmare river as a prelude to the landing at Fenit.' The geographical relationship alone makes nonsense of this statement.

8

THE WAR CONTINUES

Just ten days after the capture of Tralee, Arthur Griffith died in Dublin. An even more shattering blow lay ahead. On 22 August, Michael Collins was killed in an ambush at Béal na Bláth in County Cork. Wearily the Civil War dragged on.

By the end of August it was clear that the Republicans had lost the war. The Free State Army was dominant by reason of its numbers and resources, allied to the fact that it was the established regular army of the government in power. Moreover, its cause was accepted by the great majority of the people.

Although vastly depleted by capture and casualties, the Republicans were in no mood to accept defeat. Driven from the towns and defences they had held, they fell back on familiar guerilla warfare and seemed capable of keeping it going for years, especially from their remote strongholds in the mountainous regions of Cork and Kerry. Their strike forces, numbering fifty to a hundred, well equipped, disciplined and with battle knowledge gained in the recent fighting, proved to be formidable foes. Once compelled to take to the hills, their *modus operandi* was to strike incessantly against Free State garrisons in town and village, attack and disrupt movement of troops engaged in search and round-up operations; generally the tactics of the IRA in the Anglo-Irish War.

On 4 August, Michael Hogan, having left fifty of his 1st Westerns in Listowel, set out for Tralee with 150 men. The combined force of Dublin Guards, 1st Western troops and Eamon Horan's local men, under the overall command of O'Daly, advanced against Castleisland and, with the persuasive support of half a dozen shrapnel shells from the 18-pounder, entered the east Kerry capital and set up a number of strong posts. Hartnett's Hotel became the local headquarters.

Mick McGlynn had already moved in to the Castleisland sector. He had participated in the stiff resistance to the Free State advance on the town and, under Humphrey Murphy, was now involved in a reorganization of the Republican troops in the area. Several strike forces were immediately formed from available members of the 1st (Tralee) and 7th (Castleisland) Battalions, with a stiffening of seasoned fighting men who had hurried home to Kerry from various positions in Liam Lynch's now disrupted defence line. 'We re-established our old system of guerilla warfare,' McGlynn recalled, 'and had a busy time attacking the Staters as they tried to maintain communications by road with Castleisland. We also had a very active unit operating between Castleisland and Farranfore.'

On Sunday, 6 August, a lorry on its way from Tralee with provisions for the troops stationed in Castleisland was ambushed at Knockeen cross-roads by a strike force drawn from the two battalions, and, in the exchange of fire, Brian Houlihan of the Dublin Guards was shot dead and a number of privates were wounded. A native of Kenmare, Brian Houlihan joined the Volunteers in 1914, fought in the 1916 Rising, and was severely wounded during the subsequent Anglo-Irish War. As a result of his wounds, he was hospitalized for two years and lost the use of his right hand. The post at the workhouse in Tralee was immediately named 'Brian Houlihan Barracks' in memory of that gallant officer.

That same day, I was given a dispatch by Brigadier O'Daly in Ballymullen barracks, with instructions to take it by car to General O'Duffy in Limerick and bring back a reply with all possible speed. The car provided for the journey was an ordinary unmarked Chevrolet touring model. Four of us, including the driver, travelled under the protection of a Red Cross flag, ostensibly to obtain medical supplies in Limerick. This was not in accord with the rules of the Geneva Convention; but neither was the shooting down of the young Free State stretcher bearer, Patrick Harding, in Rock Street, Tralee, a few days earlier as he attended to our wounded under the protection of a Red Cross flag.

Our route, known to the driver (to us a journey through

uncharted territory swarming with Republican troops), was
via Castleisland, Abbeyfeale, Newcastlewest, Rathkeale and
Adare to Limerick. The dispatch was pinned inside my shirt
At first I did not display the large Red Cross flag that I carried
I was hoping that, although in uniform, we might be mistaken
for civilians if observed by hostile forces from a distance, rather
than be confronted at close quarters by troops guarding a road
block. On the Abbeyfeale road, at a point about a mile outside
Castleisland, fire was opened on us from an ambush position
sited on our left. I immediately raised the Red Cross flag aloft
and urged our driver to step hard on the gas, for I had little
illusion as to what would happen to me if caught with a
concealed dispatch in such circumstances. A momentary
cessation of fire marked the surprise appearance of the flag,
sufficient to allow us to speed clear of the bullets that
venomously pursued us because of our failure to halt.

We reached Limerick safely and I handed my dispatch to
O'Duffy's second in command, W. R. E. Murphy, at command
headquarters in Cruise's Hotel. There was a reply which I
believe had to do with the further movement of O'Daly's forces
from Tralee, and with it we set out on the return journey.
Our Chevrolet broke down in Newcastlewest. There were
troops from Dublin in the town, which had only recently been
taken from the Republicans. Looking around I saw Colonel-
Commandant Tom Kehoe sitting in a car and studying a map
with another well-known officer, Donncadh O'Hannigan, who
had been commandant of the East Limerick Brigade flying
column in the war with the British. Kehoe, a County Wicklow
man, had been a notable member of the Squad. His presence
in the Newcastle zone was typical of Collins's strategy of placing
his most dependable fighting officers in key leadership positions
in the drive southwards over land, as he had also done for
the sea-borne landings. Other officers of like quality, men such
as Jim Slattery, Tom Flood, Frank Thornton and Frank Bolster,
were stretched across the battle zone in this area to give forceful
leadership wherever it was needed.

I approached Kehoe, whom I knew, told him of my
predicament and said I had to get back urgently to Brigadier
O'Daly in Tralee. He thought for a moment. The mention

of O'Daly would stir him, I felt. They had been close comrades in the Squad and here was a chance for him to meet the brigadier in Tralee. I recall his words clearly: 'If you're not afraid of being shot,' he said, 'get into the car and I'll take you there.' We got to Tralee without incident. All through the journey, he sat beside his driver comrade, Donncadh O'Hannigan, a Peter the Painter held ready for instant action. I never heard what became of my three comrades in Newcastlewest, or what they thought of my sudden and unexplained disappearance. It was that kind of war.

The Republicans had achieved some limited local success, notably at Dundalk where fortunes swayed in seesaw fashion since the capture of the important military barracks by Free State troops in a surprise move against Commandant-General Frank Aiken's neutral 4th Northern Division on 16 July. Aiken, although recognizing the authority of GHQ in Beggars' Bush and having his troops paid by the Provisional Government, had concealed the arms of his division in secret dumps when ordered to use them against old comrades on the Republican side. The war of brothers was abhorrent to him and he had sought to persuade both sides to cease fighting each other.

Having failed to achieve a truce, he wanted to avoid involvement with either side. Commandant-General Dan Hogan of the Free State 5th Northern Division saw Aiken's policy as an exercise in benign neutrality where related to the Republican forces in the area; from his viewpoint the 4th Northern was a Free State division whose loyalty to the Provisional Government was suspect at best. He regarded Aiken as a potentially dangerous neighbour and, entirely on his own initiative, directed the action against his divisional headquarters on 16 July. Aiken, to his intense surprise and disgust, was made a prisoner, together with 300 unarmed men of his division. But not for long. On the 27th, a local Republican unit under Commandant McKenna blew a breach in the jail wall and Aiken and most of his men made a sensational escape.

Aiken was bent on recovering his headquarters and on 16 August, with assistance from McKenna, he recaptured the military barracks, and also took the other Free State posts in Dundalk in a brilliantly conceived operation that was carried out with panache. In the process, the assault troops made a huge haul of arms and ammunition. They also acquired some 300 prisoners whom they locked up in the jail, from which they released upwards of 200 Republican prisoners. The strength of the combined force under Aiken was less than 100, armed with rifles, Thompson guns and explosives. Free State casualties were severe, with five dead and about a dozen wounded. The Republicans lost McKenna, killed by the accidental detonation of one of Aiken's mines.

Three days later, on the approach of two columns of Hogan's troops, Aiken withdrew his men from Dundalk with some difficulty. In the subsequent guerilla warfare he never made significant use of the well-armed force he had at his command on the Republican side.

Tom 'Scarteen' O'Connor, in overall command of the Free State forces in south Kerry, was weakly extended. The towns he held — Kenmare, Cahirciveen and Waterville — were separated from each other by territory through which Republican forces moved without hindrance. The situation was causing him serious concern, as was the fact that of his total force of some 250 officers and men, very few, other than the small northern contingent that was with him, had received any military training whatsoever. For the greater part, his troops were local lads, most of them raw recruits; some of them drank too much and were not partial to discipline. Tough Dublin Guards, under Commandant-General Fionan Lynch, on their way from Killarney to reinforce him, were ambushed and held up by a strike force of Kerry No 2 Brigade Republicans and forced to take what cover they could find in territory that was made to measure for guerilla operations.

Lynch, who represented the South Kerry Constituency in the Dáil, was himself pinned down behind some rocks. Sharing the shelter with him, while heavy fire from positions on high ground hammered chunks out of the rocks, was Commandant Stan Bishop, who had been an early member of the Dublin Active Service Unit. 'Now then, Fionan,' exclaimed Bishop, as bullets buzzed about. 'Get out there and talk to your constituents. They seem anxious to meet you.' The general's response was not recorded, but the story became army lore, illustrative of the free and easy relationship that then prevailed between the ranks, especially among officers with pre-Truce service. What mattered that day was that the Free State column was forced to return to base in Killarney. O'Connor's positions remained precarious.

On 9 September a strike force from Brigadier John Joe Rice's Kerry No 2 Brigade, with Sean Hyde in command, infiltrated Kenmare in the early morning and recaptured the town from the garrison, which was under the command of Captain Swayne. As a preliminary to the attack, Tom O'Connor and his younger brother John were shot dead in the family home at 5 Main Street. John was in a big bed in a first-floor room, nursing a heavy cold. Tom, who had been out on a round-up, got in beside him to snatch a few hours' sleep. His orderly occupied a bed in the same room. Some Free State troops were quartered on the second floor, and two young girls occupied another room on the same floor. The girls were Kathleen Moriarty, aged nineteen, and her twelve-year old cousin, Nora O'Sullivan, a relative of the O'Connors.

About 6.30 that morning, at least five and possibly six men of the Republican force, two wearing Free State Army tunics, slipped quietly into the house through the bakery at the rear. This was easily managed without attracting attention, as No 5 opened early for the bakery business; in addition it was an open business house and there was coming and going of Free State Army personnel at all hours. What followed was indelibly printed in the mind of Nora O'Sullivan. According to her eyewitness account, the Scarteen brothers, taken by surprise, were dragged from the bed; each was shot between the eyebrows and through the heart. Both were unarmed. Tom was naked and John was wearing only a shirt. The loss of the Scarteens was grievous. The eyewitness account of the shooting and the identical nature of the wounds inflicted on them leave no grounds for doubt as to how they died.

Tom's reputation as a man of action in the war with the British is legendary. His courage and determination and his ability to rally and lead men by example was seen as a dangerous threat to the Republican cause in south Kerry.

The battle for Kenmare ended in the late afternoon with the surrender of all Free State posts in the town — the National Bank, the library, the workhouse and some other houses. It was a serious setback, and at least one hundred rifles and about 20,000 rounds of .303 ammunition had also changed hands.

Were it not for the murder of the Scarteens, the Republicans would have had good reason to be pleased with their day's work. In the event many in the strike force were deeply upset by what had happened in the house at 5 Main Street that morning, none more so than Tommy Mac and Johnny Connor, both with impeccable Anglo-Irish war records. Tommy Mac made a point of calling at the house in the evening to express his regret and sympathy to the two girls who had witnessed the foul deed. Many years afterwards, in the fifties, Johnny Connor marched in the parade to the unveiling of a memorial to the Scarteens in Kenmare.

Some days after the killing of the Scarteen O'Connors and the loss of Kenmare, the Free State forces were dealt another heavy blow. Colonel-Commandant Tom Keogh and eight comrade soldiers were blown to bits by a booby-trapped mine on a bridge at a place called Carrigaphooka in the Muskery region of County Cork. He was leading a column from Macroom to link up with Paddy O'Daly in Kerry. The booby-trapped mine is an ugly instrument of war, and the devastating effect of the blast triggered off at Carrigaphooka so early in the Civil War was felt far beyond the bounds of Muskery. Tom Keogh had been very close to Collins in Dublin. He, as a Squad man, had been through the Anglo-Irish war with a number of senior officers now serving in Kerry.

In September also, a sustained attack lasting more than thirty hours by a Republican strike force against the Free State 1st Western (Clare) garrison in Killorglin failed to break a sturdy defence which was aided by a relief force that Michael Hogan led out from Tralee. Kerrymen under Eamon Horan were with Hogan's troops. Sean Hyde, of the 1st Southern divisional staff, and Jack Flynn, the local battalion OC were in charge of the Republican force; they suffered severe casualties in killed and wounded and twenty men were captured. Some of Hogan's force were wounded.

Mindful of the ugly turn taken by the war, Horan was concerned for the safety of the prisoners. He counted all twenty as they were distributed among the lorries before the long column of the relief force started on its return to Tralee some days after the action. He was anxious about one of them, Jack Galvin of the Killorglin battalion. He had been beaten up while under interrogation by some of Michael Hogan's officers, who claimed he had shot a Free State officer near the bridge at Castlemaine, and had a broken arm. On the way back to Tralee the prisoners were ordered down from the lorries to clear a road block. Galvin, because of his injury, was not called upon to go with them. He remained under guard in his lorry. When the column arrived in Ballymullen barracks only nineteen prisoners lined up to be counted again. Galvin was missing and unaccounted for. Next day his body was found in a roadside ditch on the Killorglin road near Tralee. He had been shot dead, no doubt by officers whose duty it was to guard him.

Chivalry and humanity were early casualties on both sides in the Civil War. A young medical orderly named Lydon, a native of County Mayo, was shot dead by a Republican sniper, firing from nearby Blennerville bridge, as he cycled out the canal road from Tralee. Lydon was in uniform and wearing a Red Cross armlet. On the other side prisoners were being shot out of hand by Free State officers.

Kevin O'Higgins was angered by Free State Army excesses and was consistently and severely critical of any lapse of discipline. He had no time for apologists who tended to turn a blind eye to criminal actions by the troops. This led to friction between him and Richard Mulcahy, who defended his officers, asserting extreme provocation. The Army authorities claimed that Republican troops, having ambushed patrols and convoys and inflicted casualties, were surrendering as prisoners of war. They pointed to an episode that had occurred on 28 July when Commandant Jack Collison and Commandant-General Austin MacCurtain were killed and a divisional engineer named Powell was severely wounded in an ambush near Abbeyleix. The entire Republican column then surrendered. Collison had been commandant of the North Tipperary flying column, in which

MacCurtain had also fought, in the Anglo-Irish war.

Sweeping emergency powers sought for the Free State Army were agreed by the Cabinet, but only after prolonged and earnest consideration. The powers were granted by the Dáil on 27 September against opposition, mainly by the Labour Party which held seventeen of the 128 seats. With effect from 17 October, the Army had full power (the Army Emergency Powers) to set up secret military courts to deal with offences that included aiding and abetting an attack on the Army; arson, looting or the destruction of private or public property; being in unauthorized possession of arms, ammunition or explosives; or committing a breach of general orders or regulations made by the Army authorities. The courts could inflict the punishment of fine, imprisonment or death. Authority to execute prisoners captured bearing arms was, in fact, the power sought by the Army. An amnesty offered by the Provisional Government on 3 October remained open until the 15th of that month to 'all those engaged in insurrection and rebellion against the state' who surrendered their arms to the Free State Army and ceased to aid or abet armed opposition to the Provisional Government. 'Armed opposition' was considered to be rebellion and not war. Professor Eoin MacNeill, Minister for Education, made the point clear: 'This is not war for the republic,' he wrote editorially in *The Free State*, 'It is a rebellion against the Treaty.'

On 24 November, Erskine Childers and four young Republican soldiers were executed by firing-squad. They were carrying arms when arrested. The execution of Childers strained the interpretation of the emergency powers to the limit. He was not a combat officer; nor was the death sentence mandatory. The tiny pearl-handled pistol of which he was found to be in 'unauthorized possession' was a present from Michael Collins in happier times. Some prisoners subsequently captured with service rifles in their possession were given prison sentences; one was Paddy O'Connor, OC of the Ardfert Battalion.

Republican reaction to the executions took the form of a threat to the Dáil members who had voted for the emergency powers. In a letter to the Speaker dated 27 November, the Chief of Staff, General Liam Lynch, charged that every member of 'the illegal assembly over which you preside' who voted for the emergency powers was guilty of murder. Claiming that the Republican Army had at all times adhered to the rules of war, he warned the Speaker that 'unless your army recognizes the rules of warfare in future, we shall adopt very drastic measures to protect our forces.' Three days later he issued instructions to all commanding officers of his battalions, listing fourteen categories of persons who were to be shot at sight. At the top of the list were the Dáil members who had voted for the Army Emergency Powers resolution. They were followed by certain senators, judges of the High Court, aggressive Free State supporters and hostile newspaper men. The homes and businesses of all listed categories were to be destroyed. The Orders of Frightfulness, as Lynch's instructions came to be called, were contained in a captured document. The punishments had the approval of his Acting Assistant Chief of Staff, Ernie O'Malley.

On 7 December, Deputy Sean Hales was shot dead and his companion, Padraic O Maille, the Deputy Speaker, severely wounded. They had just mounted a sidecar outside the Ormond Hotel and were on their way to a meeting of the Dáil when a party of seven men, apparently acting on the shoot-at-sight order, opened fire on them. Next morning, four of the foremost Republican leaders — Rory O'Connor, Liam Mellows, Joe McKelvey and Dick Barrett (one from each of the four provinces) — who had been prisoners since the Four Courts surrender on 30 June, were summarily shot at dawn in Mountjoy jail by order of the Free State Cabinet, as a reprisal for the assassination of Hales and as a 'solemn warning' against the carrying out of Lynch's shoot-at-sight instructions. Their execution was awful and totally illegal but no more Dáil deputies were shot.

In all, seventy-seven Republican prisoners were executed by firing-squad between 17 November 1922 and 2 May 1923 (seven in Tralee). Of these, all but the four executed by order of the Cabinet faced the firing-squads under the special powers given to the army. The Army Emergency Powers were drastic and terrible in their implementation, but the Provisional Government believed that it had no alternative but to enforce them firmly if the country were to be pulled back from the abyss of anarchy, chaos and destruction.

Commencing on 9 December, a strong Republican force under Tom Barry, with the support of the south Tipperary veterans Commandant-General Dinny Lacey, Commandants Michael Sheehan and Bill Quirke, achieved major, but again local, success in a brilliant offensive over five days in the course of which he captured Carrick-on-Suir in County Tipperary, and Callan, Mullinavat and Thomastown in County Kilkenny. Although unable to sustain the offensive, he secured a substantial quantity of arms and ammunition and demonstrated just what the Republicans might have achieved given vigorous and intelligent leadership from the onset of the war.

The fighting continued in Munster through the autumn and winter and into the spring of 1923, but it had descended to horrifying depths of human destruction on both sides. It was an ugly and shameful period in our history and none but an enemy can record it with any satisfaction. To meet the national emergency, a large army had to be hastily created by the Provisional Government. In some areas, the state of discipline and organization in the new army was far from satisfactory. The atrocious war crimes of which certain officers of the Dublin Guards and Oriel House men were guilty in Kerry would burn in the mind for generations. In an atmosphere of hatred and anger, prisoners were beaten when under interrogation. Many were shot out of hand when surrendering. Four prisoners under the death sentence in Tralee (Cornelius Casey, Matthew Moroney and Jeremiah O'Connor, all of Tralee, and Thomas Devane of Dingle) were, for a period of six weeks, kept under suspended sentence as hostages against attack. Notices were published with effect from 21 December 1922, warning that the death sentence on each would be carried out immediately after any hostile action against the Free State troops of the Kerry command or after any interference with railways or roads or private property in the command area.

Action against the railways was crucial to the Republican Army's strategy of general destruction of public services on a nation-wide scale aimed at making the country ungovernable.

Rails were lifted, trains derailed, bridges blown up and efforts made to prevent the railway workers from running the trains. Dispatches intercepted when on their way between Liam Lynch and Ernie O'Malley reveal the importance that both attached to effecting 'the complete destruction of rail communications'. There was no question of restricting the campaign to 'trains which are assisting the enemy'. A letter dated 5 August 1922 from Ernie O'Malley's headquarters in Dublin threatened to shoot railway and other public service workers for carrying out their duties, which he construed as collaborating with the Provisional Government. The letter was read out and those responsible for it were denounced by E. P. Hart of the Amalgamated Transport and General Workers Union at the Annual Conference of the Irish Labour Party and Trades Union Council, which opened in Dublin two days later. Nevertheless, many railway workers were warned of reprisals unless they ceased co-operating with the Free Staters.

The campaign against the railways took a sinister turn in Kerry during the winter of 1922-23. It was also marked by tragedy. A group of armed men who held up a goods train at the Bog Road bridge, three miles from Tralee railway station, in December 1922, had no thought for public safety. The train had been on its way from Killarney to Tralee. One of the men summoned the fireman down off the footplate, then ordered the driver, Paddy Lennox, to send the train into Tralee without its crew. Driver Lennox refused. He said he would not be responsible for murder. The man who seemed to be the leader of the group then climbed on to the engine cab and opened the valve that released the train on a free run into Tralee, completely out of control.

Meanwhile, at Tralee station, Signalman Maurice Dore had the points set for the goods yard. Shunter Jerome O'Connor was ready to hold the handpoints for the loop that would just allow the train on to the line called 'the carriage road', where it would be brought to a halt in accordance with normal procedure. The engine would then be driven round to the rear of the train and would clear the carriage road by shunting the waggons to the goods yard. When O'Connor saw that the approaching train was not reducing speed, he realised at once that by holding the points he would sent it crashing into a gas tanker that was standing on the carriage road, immediately beneath the signal cabin and close to a public thoroughfare. The result must be a disastrous explosion. Maurice Dore and two off-duty railway men who were with him in the cabin would have little chance of surviving the blast.

O'Connor had but a few seconds to take the decision that altered the set course of the runaway train by sending it down to the store road, where seven or eight waggons were standing. Although the wagons took the brunt of the impact, as he knew they would, the train smashed them through the wall that bounded the station buildings and yards. The pile-up of engine and waggons blocked the main Tralee–Listowel road and part of the railway line, coming to rest against the first railway terrace house on the far side of the road and directly opposite the railway goods store. Most of the waggons were reduced to matchwood. Fortunately, nobody was injured in this mindless act of terrorism, carried out in the name of the republic and repeated in Newcastlewest on 6 March 1923.

Tragedy attended an attempt by a north Kerry Republican unit to derail a troop train at Liscahane bridge near Ardfert on 19 January 1923. Led by Tom Driscoll of Kilmoyley, the Republicans lifted the rails at the bridge on receipt of information that a troop train from Limerick to Tralee would be next on the line. The attempt went wrong because the troop train arrived late in Listowel and a goods train was sent to Tralee ahead of it. Driscoll, informed of the switch, had the signals set against the goods train at Ardfert and his men also fired shots in a frantic effort to stop it. The driver, Paddy Riordan, may have thought that an attempt was being made to seize the train, as had happened in December at the Bog Road bridge on the far side of Tralee. He ignored the signal, probably because of the shooting, and he and his fireman, Dan Crowley were scalded to death when the engine toppled over the bridge.

Strong and widespread condemnation of the Republican campaign of destruction followed the train episode at the Bog Road bridge and was repeated after the tragic occurrence at Liscahane bridge. I believe it was the people's outspoken rejection of such methods of waging war that prompted the crime which followed on 23 January. That evening an engine driver was shot dead and another slightly wounded. The Kerry command of the Free State Army alleged that they were shot because they had refused to co-operate with the Republicans in the wrecking of trains and other railway property.

The *Weekly Freeman* of 27 January reported the shooting as follows:

> While engine drivers Dan Daly and Dan Lynch were chatting on the roadside outside Tralee railway station at 7.30 last (Tuesday) evening after shunting operations, two men wearing trench coats accosted them. 'Are you Daly?' asked one. 'Are you Lynch?' queried the other. The drivers answered affirmatively. The accosters drew revolvers and fired point blank. Daly died; Lynch escaped with slight wounds.
>
> These outrages are counter-productive, as, in addition to the opprobrium which they brought on the anti-Treatite cause, railwaymen in Tralee met and issued a statement that, although they had received letters threatening them with death ... neither murder nor assassination would prevent them from carrying out their duties and what the Black and Tans had failed to accomplish, the wreckers would also fail to achieve.

In fact, Daly and Lynch were shot by three Free State officers. Without knowing their intent, I saw them leave the workhouse where I was stationed, to carry out the crime. I also saw them return. They were not in uniform and they wore trench coats.

Free State intelligence officers stationed at Hartnett's Hotel in Castleisland had a bad reputation for ill-treatment of prisoners, including torture during interrogation. Republicans identified one officer in particular and accused him of gross brutality to prisoners.

Officers of the 7th (Castleisland) Battalion, Kerry No 1 Brigade, discovered that information on members of the battalion and their movements was being mailed to a Free

State officer by a woman residing near the village of Knocknagoshel. They had intercepted one of her letters. The discovery led to a horrifying sequence of murderous episodes that shocked the entire country.

Against the advice of his comrades, a senior officer of the battalion insisted on the discovery being used to lure the intelligence officer to death by trip mine. A report in writing, which resembled that of the letters reaching Hartnett's Hotel from the informant, was left in Castleisland for the Free State officer by a woman courier acting for the Republicans. It informed him that local members of the Republican Army were sleeping in a newly made dug-out in a field a couple of miles from Knocknagoshel village. A powerful mine, made by two battalion officers on the orders of the superior officer, was left by them in a wooden box in what looked like the entrance to an underground dug-out at the point indicated in the report. The mine was set for instantaneous explosion and any attempt to move or lift the box would detonate it. After midnight on the night of 5 March a number of officers from Hartnett's Hotel took a detail of troops out to the dug-out on a search mission. The Free State officer at the core of the affair, two captains and two privates were blown to pieces. The sequel was even more appalling.

Reprisals for the mine were deliberately planned by a clique of influential Dublin Guards officers in Ballymullen barracks and carried out in the vicinity of Tralee, Killarney and Cahirciveen. In the early hours of Wednesday, 7 March, nine Republican prisoners were removed from where they were being held in the Tralee workhouse and taken under military escort in an army lorry to a point near Ballyseedy Cross, some two miles distant. There they were bound hand and foot and roped together in a circle, their backs to a log and some loose stones, beneath which a mine had been placed. Eight were blown to bits. In the course of the morning their remains were released, in nine coffins, to their families. The condition of the bodies was such that there was no way of knowing that one of the nine had been blown clear with only minor injuries. He was Stephen Fuller of Fahernan, Kilflynn, and his name was on one of the coffins.

Shoftly afterwards, four Republican prisoners were murdered in the same foul manner at Countess Bridge, Killarney. Five had been taken out to die, and again one escaped — Stephen Coffey of Barlemaint. The crimes were repeated on 12 March, when five prisoners were taken from the workhouse near Cahirciveen. There was no survivor.

An official army statement was issued on 8 March as follows:

A party of troops proceeding from Tralee to Killorglin last night came across a barricade of stones built on the roadway at Ballyseedy bridge. The troops returned to Tralee and brought a number of prisoners to remove the obstruction. While engaged in the work a trigger mine (which was concealed) exploded, wounding Captain Breslin, Lieutenant Murtagh, Sergeant Ennis and killing eight prisoners.

On another bridge the troops found a barricade similar to that at Ballyseedy bridge erected across the roadway. While the obstruction was being removed a trigger mine exploded, wounding two of the troops and killing four irregular prisoners who had been engaged in removing the barricade.

The facts are that the mines used in the slaughter of the prisoners were constructed in Tralee under the supervision of two senior Dublin Guards officers. An alleged military court of enquiry into the occurrences was held in Tralee on 7 April 1923; the submission made to the court and the findings brought in are, to my personal knowledge, totally untrue.

It is unknown how many Republican prisoners paid for the Knocknagoshel mine with their lives. The last was Jerh O'Leary, OC of the 7th Battalion. Captured in a farmhouse near Knocknagoshel after Frank Aiken's cease fire order of 24 May 1923, he was taken to Castleisland and murdered in Hartnett's Hotel next morning. As far as can be ascertained, officers set him up for what was designed to look like an attempt at escape. One of them shot him in the back.

In the midst of darkness a dawning ray of hope had already appeared. The Deputy Chief of Staff of the Republican Army, Liam Deasy, had been captured in arms on 18 January and sentenced to death in Clonmel. He had earlier arrived at a personal conviction that the war should end and now sought the permission of his captors to communicate his views to his military colleagues, not as an attempt to save his own life, but in a genuine realization of the disaster that faced the nation by a continuance of the unnatural conflict. He was permitted to do this, but only after he had agreed to sign a document dictated by Richard Mulcahy in the form of an undertaking 'to accept and aid in an immediate and unconditional surrender of all arms and men'. Copies of this document, together with a long letter in which he courageously gave his reasons for signing it, were sent out on 29 January to Republican military and political leaders named in the document. Liam Lynch replied formally and coldly on behalf of the Republican Army and underground Government that 'the proposal contained in your circular letter of 30 January, and the enclosure cannot be considered'.

Most other members of the Republican Executive believed as Deasy did, and the thought of peace grew with the passing weeks. Deasy was not executed. A meeting of the Executive, which had been forced from place to place in County Waterford in the period 23-26 March by raiding Free State troops, ended indecisively in the Nire valley on the 26th, but the realization of the futility of prolonged conflict was growing. A proposal by Tom Barry 'that in the opinion of the Executive further armed resistance and operations against the Free State government will not further the cause of the independence of the country' was narrowly defeated, by six votes to five. One of the six was Liam Lynch, now Acting Commander-in-Chief as well as Chief of Staff of the Republican Army. Despite heavy losses and other disasters, he was determined to continue with the war until the Provisional Government was forced to negotiate. His optimistic view of the military situation found very little acceptance. Only two members of the Executive of the 1st Southern Division felt that some prospect of military victory remained; they were the OCs of Kerry No 2 and Cork No 3, John Joe Rice and Ted O'Sullivan. But of the members at the March meeting, all but Lynch believed that the military effort had failed and that the war should be brought to an end. How to end it was the only question that divided them.

On the morning of 10 April, General Lynch fell mortally wounded in a pass through the Knockmealdown mountains. Accompanied by six members of the Executive, he had been on his way to a meeting that would consider whether they should fight on, surrender, or dump arms and simply quit. As he saw the options, his own course was clear: he had declared for an Irish Republic and remained determined to live under no other law. With his death the end of Republican resistance was very near. Further meetings of the Executive and the underground Republican Government took place, and on 24 May Frank Aiken, now Chief of Staff, ordered his forces to cease fire and dump arms.

An engagement at Clashmealcon caves was the last major episode of the war in Kerry. About mid-April, Timothy (Aeroplane) Lyons and five members of his scattered North Kerry Republican column holed up in Dumfort's cave, one of the Clashmealcon caves, deep down in a tall cliff facing the turbulent Atlantic off Kerry Head. It was a poor choice of a place of refuge, for there was no escape from the cave, and the men were trapped inside by units of Michael Hogan's 1st Western Division. Two Free State soldiers were shot dead from the cave, and, under the Army Emergency Powers, that almost certainly sealed the fate of the men inside. Two of the column, Tommy McGrath and Pat O'Shea, were drowned while attempting to escape on the night of 16 April. Lyons himself surrendered on the morning of the 18th but the rope on which he was being hauled up to the cliff's edge broke and he fell back down on to the rocks below. His body was riddled with bullets by the troops above. The remaining members of the group, Reginald Hathaway, Edward Greaney and James McEnery, also surrendered and were brought up. All three were sentenced to death and were executed in Ballymullen barracks, Tralee, on 25 April.

The physical war was over, but rumblings of conflict remained for a long time. It was not easy to erase from bitter minds the hatreds engendered and sustained in the year just gone. The cost had been bitter too. By grim coincidence, the Commanders-in-Chief of both armies, Michael Collins and Liam Lynch, were dead, each killed by a single isolated shot. Dead, too, were Cathal Brugha and Michael Collins's close friend, Harry Boland, as were a great many others on both sides, rank and file whose names had long been associated in the public mind with the Independence movement of 1916-21. An estimated four thousand dead and wounded, thirteen thousand Republicans in captivity and some seventeen million pounds in destruction completed the picture of the Free State torn apart in the year of fratricidal strife.

Some elements that attached themselves to the Republicans engaged in wanton destruction of property almost everywhere. The loss to the country was enormous, as historic mansions and castles were blown up or burned down with their priceless treasures in manuscripts, books and art collections, apparently for no reason other than that their owners had belonged to the former unionist ascendancy.

EPILOGUE

In Kerry, veterans of that time will tell you that their hearts were not in the Civil War. They will talk, too, of Michael Collins and express a strong belief that he was assassinated by one of his own at Béal na Bláth, because he sought peace with his opponents when others wanted war; a preposterous suggestion, totally against reason and fact. That they persist in the claim shows in itself the appeal that Michael Collins held in the hearts of men who fought on opposite sides in the Civil War.

These veterans talk with justifiable bitterness about the Free State murder of prisoners at Ballyseedy, Countess Bridge, Killarney and Cahirciveen, but make no mention of the Republican trap mine at Macroom, or that of Knocknagoshel which led directly to the Free State mines. Yet they have every reason to feel bitter about the horrific war in Kerry in 1922-23. They suffered greatly.

Time diminishes memory even if it cannot erase it and one can only hope that their memories of these events will take the form of a rejection of man's inhumanity to man wherever it exists in our land today for whatever reason.

Not so very long ago I walked the pier at Fenit in the company of men who had opposed our landing and continued their armed opposition long afterwards. We could discuss the effective range of a .303 Lee Enfield rifle or a Lewis gun, the weapons of the time. And we could try to estimate the distance from pier to shore, across water; and we could recall too, the shock effect of a Vickers machine-gun in full blast. Enemies on that battleground of half a century ago, we could discuss these things, calmly and reflectfully — without rancour!

But we could also turn away from such thinking and live

this day, forgetting the past, and see before us and all around us the beauty of a sunlit Tralee bay, with distant bathers along the shore and colourful yachts skimming the sea, while foreign visitors stood happily, and perhaps fruitlessly, rod fishing at the end of the pier.

We could look upon this scene on a summer day and say very truthfully that here, indeed, was peace.

And then we could go back thoughtfully to the Spa and enjoy a drink together at Micheal Lynch's Bar.

NOTES AND SOURCES

1 Papers of General Richard Mulcahy, Archives Department, University College, Dublin.
2 Commandant-General Tom Barry. *The Reality of the Anglo-Irish War 1920-21 in West Cork* (Dublin, 1974), 52.
3 *Ibid.*
4 David Fitzpatrick, *Politics and Irish Life 1913-21* (Dublin, 1977), 224.
5 Florence O'Donoghue, *No Other Law* (Dublin, 1954), 176.
6 Charles Townshend, *The British Campaign in Ireland 1919-21* (Oxford, 1975), 192 and fn. 66, quoting Memo 'B' by General Officer Commanding-in-Chief Ireland, 23 May 1921, in memo by Chief Imperial General Staff, 24 May 1921, CP 2965, CAB 24 123 (Records of the Cabinet Office, in the Public Record Office, London).
7 Thomas Jones, *Whitehall Diary* (ed. Keith Middlemas), vol III, Ireland 1918-1925 (London, 1971), 73. The greater part of this narrative is concentrated on the making of the Anglo-Irish Treaty in 1921, and is a remarkable primary source for historians. Jones, a confidant of Lloyd George, was Assistant Secretary to the British Cabinet, 1916-1930.
8 C.J.C. Street, *Ireland in 1921* (London, 1922), 47. Street was supervisor of the publicity section of the Irish Office in London. His first book, *The Administration of Ireland in 1920* (London, 1921), was published under the pseudonym of 'IO'. Both books are packed with quotations from police and other documents and can to this extent be regarded as primary sources.
9 Townshend, *opus cit*, 196, fn 139, quoting 'G' War Diary,

GHQ Ireland, 14, 15, 16, 17, 28 July 1921, WO 35 93 (1)/1 (Records of the War Office, in the Public Record Office, London.)

10 Winston Churchill, *The Aftermath. A Sequel to the World Crisis* (London, 1941).

11 C. E. Callwell, *Field Marshal Sir Henry Wilson. His Life and Diaries* (London, 1927), vol II, 271.

12 Barry, *opus cit*. The issue of the Treaty was not put directly to the people in the election.

13 Led by Eamon de Valera, the anti-Treaty deputies ignored the summons to attend what they regarded as a meeting of the Parliament of Southern Ireland set up under the Government of Ireland Act 1920 (the Partition Act) of the British Parliament.

14 Conor Brady, *Guardians of the Peace* (Dublin, 1974), 34–35.

15 O'Donoghue, *opus cit*, 209.

16 *Ibid*, 205. See also Piaras Béaslaí, *Michael Collins and the Making of a New Ireland* (London, 1926), vol II, 367–371.

17 Ernie O'Malley, *The Singing Flame* (Dublin, 1978), 52–53.

18 O'Donoghue, *opus cit*, 18.

19 Mulcahy Papers.

20 O'Donoghue, *opus cit*, 205.

21 Churchill, Colonial Secretary, in the House of Commons, 7 March 1922, in reply to a question by Sir William Davison.

22 O'Donoghue, *opus cit*, 207.

23 *Ibid*, 215.

24 *Ibid*, 217.

25 Dorothy Macardle, *The Irish Republic* (London, 1937), 706.

26 O'Donoghue, *opus cit*, 220–224.

27 William O'Brien, *Forth the Banners Go* (Dublin, 1969), 219–220. See also P. S. O'Hegarty, *The Victory of Sinn Féin* (London, 1924), 86–7.

28 O'Brien, *opus cit*, 219–220, for a statement by Cathal Brugha to Michael Collins on wading through the blood

of Irish ministers.

29 For more on de Valera's attitude to the Treaty see E. MacLysaght, *Changing Times in Ireland since 1898* (London, 1972), 127–131.

30 Until the repeal of the External Relations Act 1936, on 18 April 1949, the Free State had retained a tenuous link with the British Crown and Commonwealth.

31 Eoin Neeson, *The Civil War in Ireland 1921–23* (Cork, 1966), 59. Official British sources put the quantity of arms seized at 381 rifles, 727 revolvers, thirty-three Lewis guns, six Maxim guns and 25,000 rounds of ammunition.

32 De Valera, at Killarney, 19 March 1922.

33 O'Donoghue, *opus cit*, 224.

34 Macardle, *opus cit*, 724.

35 O'Donoghue, *opus cit*, 230.

36 Macardle, *opus cit*, 724.

37 Béaslaí, *opus cit*, 384.

38 O'Malley, *opus cit*, 67.

39 Robert Kee, *The Green Flag* (London, 1972), 737.

40 O'Donoghue, *opus cit*, 236.

41 *Ibid*, 236.

42 Dan Breen, *My Fight for Irish Freedom*, Anvil edition (Dublin, 1981), 184.

43 *Ibid*, 182.

44 *Ibid*, 185.

45 *Ibid*, 184–85.

46 O'Donoghue, *opus cit*, 238.

47 Béaslaí, *opus cit*, 393, quoting from an interview given by Michael Collins to John S. Steele of the *Chicago Tribune*, 15 May 1922.

48 Michael Collins, *The Path to Freedom* (Dublin, 1922), 16–18.

49 Macardle, *opus cit*, 238–9.

50 O'Donoghue, *opus cit*, 244.

51 *Ibid*, 243–44.

52 *Ibid*, 245.

53 The quotations are from 'Extract from a notebook, the property of Seán MacBride,' in *Survivors*, 'The Story of Ireland's struggle as related to Uinseann MacEoin by some

of her outstanding living people,' (Dublin, 1980) 126–130.
54 O'Donoghue, *opus cit*, 245.
55 *Ibid*, 246.
56 *Ibid*, 246.
57 *Ibid*, 246.
58 *Ibid*, 246.
59 O'Hegarty, *opus cit*, 123.
60 Macardle, *opus cit*, 775.
61 *Ibid*, 775–6.
62 *Ibid*, 777.
63 Casualties suffered by the Provisional Government forces during the fighting in Dublin, as reported in the issue of the *Irish Independent* for 8 July, amounted to sixteen dead and 122 wounded.
64 Macardle, *opus cit*, 778.
65 Mulcahy Papers.
66 General Michael J. Costello has recorded that 'the numbers and proportion of the pre-Truce IRA with combat experience who took up arms against the Treaty has been grossly exaggerated. The great majority of the 1st Southern did oppose the Treaty, largely due to the influence of Liam Lynch himself. Also there was a big anti-Treaty majority in Mayo, Sligo and West Galway. In other provincial areas the overwhelming majority of the men who mattered were pro-Treaty, as were the majority and best of the fighting men in Dublin.' (Letter dated 25 July 1977 to Dan Nolan of Tralee.)
67 Richard Mulcahy, in a confidential report to Michael Collins, dated 4 August 1922. Mulcahy Papers.
68 Information from Michael (Mick) McGlynn of Tralee who participated in the actions at Listowel and Lixnaw.
69 *Ibid*.
70 No record of the strength of the National Army prior to 31 March 1923 is available. No record was kept of the number of NCOs serving during 1922–23. A fair estimate would be 'about 12,000 to 15,000'. Information from the office of the Adjutant-General, Parkgate, to the Assistant Chief of Staff, 18 May 1938 (in the Papers of Michael J. Costello in Costello family possession).

71 Information from Mick McGlynn.
72 Calton Younger, *Ireland's Civil War* (London, 1968), 370.
73 Mulcahy report to Collins, 4 August 1922.
74 *Ibid.*
75 *Ibid.*
76 *Ibid.*
77 *Ibid.*
78 Photo copy in possession of the editor.
79 Information from W. J. Clifford, London.
80 *The Kerry People*, property of Maurice Ryle and Thomas Quirke, both of Tralee, was the only newspaper published in Tralee in August 1922. On 8 September, it was suppressed by anti-Treaty forces who carried away vital parts of the printing plant. The premises of J. B. Quinnell & Sons Ltd, Russell Street, publishers of *The Kerry Weekly Reporter*, *The Kerry News* and *The Killarney Echo*, were burned by the RIC on 31 October 1920. In March 1921, Auxiliaries bombed the plant of The Kerryman Ltd., Edward Street, publishers of *The Kerryman* and *The Liberator*. The Civil War had ended before publication of the Quinnell and The Kerryman newspapers was resumed.
81 Collins, *opus cit*, 41.

APPENDIX 1

THE FIRST NATIONAL EMERGENCY

(from an examination of unpublished documents)

On 7 July 1922, the Provisional Government issued this proclamation of appeal to the Irish people.

> Events have shown that while the present active strength of the Army has been sufficient to deal adequately with the recent situation, there is the possibility of the continued sporadic action which makes an increase in the Army Establishment vitally necessary.

In addition to planning army expansion, the Government made known its intention to establish a War Council. A memorandum on the decision was addressed to Arthur Griffith, President of Dáil Éireann, by Michael Collins on 14 July:

> It would be well, I think, if the Government issued a sort of Official Instruction to me nominating the War Council of Three, and appointing me to act by special order of the Government as Commander-in-Chief during the period of hostilities.
>
> It should contain a statement which could be directed to the Army by me as an Order of the Day. The statement should cover in a general way a point that has already been covered by the statement of the Government made on the fall of the Four Courts. It should be pointed out that in the present fighting the men we have lost have died for something, that the wounded are suffering for something. That they have died and are suffering for the very same principle that we fought the British for — the People's right to live and be governed in the way they themselves choose.
>
> This should go on to deal with the point that what the

Army is fighting at present is mere brigandage, and when not this it is opposition to the People's will. What they are fighting for is the revival of the nation. That this revival and restoration of order cannot in any way be regarded as a step backwards, nor a repression, nor a reactionary step, but a clear step forward.

As was predictable, the new Commander-in-Chief moved with his accustomed speed. On 27 July, he instructed Richard Mulcahy, Chief of Staff, that a 'very urgent' report be prepared for the Government along the following lines:

(a) Our entire strength in officers, men and equipment, with a general note on the distribution.
(b) Report of casualties incurred by us.
(c) Prisoners taken by us and disposal of the person, number released, medical condition, etc.
(d) An appreciation to some extent of the decision we have to deal with yet, with an estimate of the time we are likely to take.

On August 4, General Mulcahy sent this reply:

Just at the moment it is difficult to get a definite statement with regard to our strength in officers, men and equipment, indicating their distribution. The attached schedules, however, give a general view of the situation. I have had them prepared as such, and as giving a statement which will act as a base-line from which a more correct statement may be developed.

Statement No. 1: Total number of Regulars enrolled.
Statement No. 2: Reserves allotted to the different Commands.
Statement No. 3: Approximate distribution of pre-Treaty supplies under our control.
Statement No. 4: Approximate distribution of post-Treaty supplies under our control.
Casualties: It has been difficult to get our people to report

their casualties properly. Statement No. 5 shows our minimum casualties.

Statement No. 6: Shows the position with regard to prisons on 31 July.

A commentary on the difficulties under the circumstances existing in the various Divisions of getting accurate information is the fact that the following are the latest statements of man strength that we can get from the Divisions:

1st Northern Division	850 men
Western Command	2,234 men
Eastern Command	4,175 men
South-Western Command	3,564 men
2nd Southern	1,232 men
3rd Southern	915 men
	12,970 men

This is a total figure less than the total of Regulars enrolled, namely 14,127.

As against the figures given in his own report, Major-Gen. McKeon admits that there are more than 1,000 additional men in his area that he cannot at present indicate the distribution of.

Outside the Waterford-Cork-Kerry-Limerick area, where our only definite military problem confronts us, work of rearrangement and reorganization is now going on, which will, within a fortnight or so, remedy this state of affairs. The rearrangement being carried out in the Western Command is indicated hereunder (Statement No. 7). This area comprises approximately the counties of North Galway, Mayo, Sligo, Leitrim, Roscommon, Longford, Western Cavan, portion of Westmeath. Here 30 of the present posts are being closed forthwith. The miltary establishments which will remain in the area will be 22 garrisons and 4 columns; comprising a total approximately of 2,100 men. It is proposed to withdraw from the area for training, and for service in other areas, men surplus to this number. A systematic programme of work will be gone through by the columns and garrisons remaining in the area.

The military problem in the Western area consists of dealing with 4 bodies of Irregulars, as follows:—

1. A party of about 70 under Carty, T.D., operating in the neighbourhood of Tubbercurry and Swinford. This is the only body of any vigour or of decent morale.

2. A body of about 250, operating North and South of Sligo, under Devine and Pilkington.

3. A body under Bofin, operating in the Arigna-Dromahair area. At the moment the surrender of Bofin and his party is being negotiated.

4. And a very disordered band of about 60 towards the Ballinrobe side.

Generally, there is no military problem more serious than this to be settled outside the Waterford-Cork-Kerry-Limerick area.

The Army has no further decision to take with regard to the country outside this latter area. As far as general decisions go, if the problems of this latter area did not exist, Parliament should be summoned, and the question of Police, Courts, and the necessary punishments for people found guilty of breaking railways, cutting telegraph wires, looting, carrying arms unauthorizedly, etc, settled.

The Army would simply then have to co-operate with the Police, and would be able effectively to do this. Already as regards policing in this area it is essential that the Civic Guard take up their police duties. The position in the West is that while reducing such cases to the minimum we have to retain small posts in 5 places in the Western Command, in order to prevent good police barracks being burned down. Otherwise, in connection with our scheme for organization we would withdraw our men from these posts.

In the South, the immediate military problem that confronts us is not so much the military defeat of the Irregulars in that area, as the establishing of our Forces in certain principal points in the area; with a view to shaking the domination held over the ordinary people by the Irregulars. The establishing of ourselves in a few more of these positions would mean the resurgence of the people from their cowed condition, and the realization by the Irregulars that they had lost their grip on the people and that they could not hope to last. An immediate demoralization of the Irregulars rank and file would be the result. It is too early to say yet whether we could so establish ourselves in time to have Parliament to meet on 12th (August). I feel that we shall have to have another postponement, and that even the political effect of another postponement would be good. It would confirm to the general public our determination to clean up this matter definitely, and it will have the important effect of preventing the Irregulars in the South feeling that as soon as we came definitely up against them, we hesitated to face them boldly, and turned aside from the job, and called Parliament. To risk any such idea arising in the minds of the Southern Irregulars, with the resultant rise in morale on their part, would be a very serious matter.

I consider that if Parliament did not meet until 24th our military position would be very favourable; we would have occupied sufficient additional posts in the South to dominate entirely the position there, and would be able to indicate so definitely our ability to deal with the military problem there that no parliamentary criticism of any kind could seriously interfere with our ability. Even if, in any area, there was any delay in solving any definite military problem, the Police and Court arrangements which it is expected will solve the difficulties in other parts of the country, could be introduced in the large areas in the South, and the seat of the military problem could be restricted.

Beir Beannacht,
Chief of the General Staff.

STATEMENT 1: Total number of Regulars enrolled

Command	Officers*	Men
Eastern (including Guards)		5,110
South-Western		2,850
2nd Southern } 3rd Southern }		1,550
Western		2,700
1st Northern		550
Curragh		500
GHQ and Special Services		867
Total		14,127

*The approximate number of officers included is 700.

STATEMENT 2: Reserves allotted to different Commands

Command	Number allotted
Eastern	7,450
South-Western	2,750
2nd Southern	1,000
3rd Southern	800
Western	2,300
1st Northern	1,400
Total	15,700

These are the figures allotted to the different Commands, with authority to recruit. It is not possible to state definitely that these actual numbers have been recruited, as in many of the Commands the immediate requirements, because of the hostilities in those Commands, have necessitated the absorption of the Reserves into the operating Forces. Approximately 10,000 men have been enrolled in the Reserves up to the present.

STATEMENT 3: Approximate distribution of pre-Treaty supplies under our control

Command	Rifles	Revolvers	Machine-guns
Eastern	742	1,674	15
South-Western	156	323	4
2nd Southern	—	—	—
3rd Southern	146	369	2
Western	154	345	4
1st Northern	139	148	1
Six-County	363	615	9
Total	1,700	3,474	35

STATEMENT 4: Approximate distribution of post-Treaty supplies under our control

Command	Rifles	Revolvers	Machine-guns	18 pounders	Armoured Cars
Eastern	9,459	2,272	108	2	6
South-Western	2,270	426	13	3	2
2nd Southern	1,440	322	13	1	—
3rd Southern	500	32	1	—	2
Western	2,453	170	12	2	2
1st Northern	1,000	250	5	—	—
Curragh	2,000	—	5	—	—
Six-County	938	1,215	4	—	—
Total	20,060	4,687	156	8	12

STATEMENT 5: Minimum casualties to national troops up
to 31/7/22

Area	Dead	Wounded	Reported in I. Indept.
Dublin	16	122	8 July
Tirconnell	1	1	13 July
(Snipers)	2	—	10 July
Waterford	2	1	22 July
Ambushes	2	1	18 & 19 July
Limerick	6	20	24 July
Waterford (Ambush)	1	—	24 July
Killurin (Ambush)	2	7	25 July
Galway & Tirconnell (Ambushes)	4	—	28 July
Bruree	13	—	31 July
Mayo	2	—	31 July
Leix	3	5	31 July
Dundrum	1	—	1 August
Tipperary	4	3	1 August
Total	59	160	National Army

STATEMENT 6: Prisoners in custody on 31st July, 1922

There are about 2,000 persons in military custody throughout the country as follows:

Prison	Number
Mountjoy	646
Kilmainham	190
Athlone	220
Kilkenny	200 (approx.)
Curragh	100
Wellington	100
Portobello	73
c/o Joe Sweeney	140
Lucan	16
Kilcock	3
Dundalk	187
Beggars' Bush	31
Galway	80
Total	1,786

Releases: Athlone 11. Curragh 14. Mountjoy & Kilmainham 97.

Note: There are probably a few hundred more prisoners than those given above. It is also probable that there have been very many more releases.

Author's comment: The report, which is in General Mulcahy's unsorted papers in the archives of University College, Dublin, was the first military 'estimate of the situation' by the Irish Army, and for that reason alone it must be regarded as a document of much historic interest.

According to the report, the south was the only area in need of serious military attention at 4 August 1922. This was a curiously low-key approach to a national problem of increasing bitterness, destruction and death by violence. The war would continue for another nine months, and seventy-six men would die before Free State firing-squads in areas of the north, east and west, as well as in the south.

Another feature of interest is that although the report is dated 4 August, four days after the *Lady Wicklow* expedition had left Dublin, it contains no mention whatsoever of plans for a landing of Free State troops at Fenit. Equally strange is the fact that widespread search has failed to locate an operational order or any other military directive related to the landing. There are grounds for believing, indeed, that the decision to sail was a hurried one after failure to co-ordinate plans with the Tralee Treaty supporters.

There is a strongly expressed desire in the report for the early appearance of a return to the civil procedures of law and order. This, it is said, would follow the Free State occupation of towns when members of the recently formed Civic Guard should move in to deal with civil offences against the law. The official military press instruction at that time was to play down the civil war aspect and concentrate on the role of the army as simply co-operating with the police. This much desired situation was, however, a long way ahead.

The question has to be asked as to what extent the report was intended to pacify the minds of the members, particularly the Labour members, of the prorogued Dáil when it should reassemble, as it eventually did, on 9 September. No doubt the members of that body would wish to know how the military forces of the State were handling a situation of revolt against the authority of Dáil Éireann.

The casualty list accompanying the report presents the strange spectacle of a list of that nature being compiled from newspaper reports, and not from Army medical sources. But, in fact, there were no sources which could provide a comprehensive list of dead and wounded soldiers at that particular time. The Medical Corps was a slow starter and mostly consisted of medical units, or Red Cross men as they were called. For the first months of the war doctors were provided by local contract, or by previous serving members of the IRA. It was unusual to have doctors accompany active field units. No doctors accompanied sea-borne troops at Westport, Fenit, Kenmare and Passage West. The Fenit unit had as senior medic Sergeant T. J. (Ted) Keatinge from Drogheda. The 1st Western Unit under Michael Hogan, which landed at Tarbert, had Captain (Doctor) Charlie Stewart, who was an active member of the Clare IRA, pre-Truce; he was later Colonel, Director of Army Medical Services.

APPENDIX 2

THE VOLUNTEER RESERVE

The conditions of enlistment in the Government Reserve Scheme, stated in the Mulcahy papers dated 26 July 1922, are:

It must be distinctly understood that all men who have joined the Army or who have been engaged in active service since the outbreak of hostilities, and who were not at that date attested in the Regular Army must be regarded as coming within the terms of the Government Reserve Scheme. The terms of service for such men is six months or such shorter period as the Army Council may determine.

The Scheme provides that all such men shall be drafted to the Curragh Camp for a short period of intensive training prior to being posted to the Commands as required. It is realized, however, that in all the Command areas it was found necessary to place a number of the recruits on active service at once.

All men joining since 28 June, 1922, ie, all men not in the Regular Army at that date, are to be classified as Volunteer Reserve.

A quota has been allotted to each area and when this is filled recruiting must cease.

Care must be taken in selecting recruits that no persons of bad character should be accepted.

OGLAIGH na hÉIREANN   July 1922

VOLUNTARY LEVY: APPLICATION FORM

1. I _____ wish to Volunteer for enrolment in the Volunteer Levy called for by the Government to deal with the present National Emergency.

2. Name _____ Age ____ Birthplace _____

3. Present address _____ County _____

4. Occupation _____

5. Name and address of employer _____

6. IRA record: _____

Rank Held	Period

7. Other Military Experience:

Army	Rank Held	Period

8. Special Army Qualifications (if any) _____

9. If knowledge of Irish _____

10. Other special qualifications (if any) _____

11. Married or Single _____

12. No. of children _____

Date _____ Signed _____

July 1922

OGLAIGH na hÉIREANN
VOLUNTEER RESERVE
AGREEMENT FORM

I _____

of _____

in the County of _____ do hereby agree and offer
to serve as a soldier of the Irish Republican Army Volunteer
Reserve for a period of six months, or such shorter period
as may be determined by the Army Council. In return for
my service I do agree to accept the allowances hereinunder
described.

I do further agree to obey the orders issued or promulgated
to me by superior officers and, should I commit a breach of
discipline, to accept such punishment as may be determined
by my superior officers in accordance with the disciplinary
code now administered in the Regular Army.

The following are the rates of pay:

All ranks: Three shillings and sixpence per day and
Maintenance.

The following are the rates of Dependants' Allowances:

Wife   – Four shillings per day.
Wife and Child   – Five shillings and sixpence per day.
Wife and Two Children   – Six shillings and sixpence per day.
Wife and Three Children   – Seven shillings and threepence per
                                     day.

I do agree that Dependants' Allowance be paid to my wife
and that her signature be accepted as sufficient receipt.

Signature of Person Offering Service

Date _____   _____

Rank _____

APPENDIX 3

VESSELS SUITABLE AND AVAILABLE

AS TROOP TRANSPORTS

On 15 July 1922, General Richard Mulcahy wrote to the Commander-in-Chief, General Michael Collins, from Portobello barracks, enclosing 'a list of Vessels which can be made available as Troop Transports, for your information':

List of Vessels Class 1. (Miscellaneous Vessels)
named on 9 July 1922

Vessel	Gross Tonnage	Dimensions	Draft	Accommodate
Ulster	2,641	360 x 41	16	1,800
Munster	2,641	346 x 41	16	1,500
Arvonia	2,641	329 x 39	12	1,500
Cambria	2,641	387 x 45	15	2,000
Hibernia	3,458	380 x 45	14	2,000
Anglia	3,053	380 x 45	14	2,000
Scotia	3,300	387 x 45	15	2,000
Galtee More	3,300	387 x 45	15	1,000
Rathmore	1,569	299 x 37	13	1,000
Slieve Gallion	1,071	299 x 35	14	1,000

The owner in each case was the City of Dublin Steam Packet Company.

The *Lady Wicklow*, not included in this list, was much engaged in the evacuation of British forces and was probably not available at the time it was being prepared by the Department of Economics.

174

APPENDIX 4

THE SQUAD AND THE

DUBLIN ACTIVE SERVICE UNIT

In Dublin, the G (Political) Division of the Dublin Met-
ropolitan Police (DMP) was a specially trained branch of the
force. The G-men knew the city area thoroughly, the city IRA
officers and members of Dáil Éireann, and guided by RIC
information they followed all outstanding men who came up
from the country. As was true of the country districts, British
regular army Intelligence officers in Dublin had little or no
intimate knowledge of wanted men; they were guided by DMP
information. In this way, the work of the armed plain clothes
detectives of the G Division constituted a menace to the entire
independence movement, for if the Government of the Republic
and the IRA organization in Dublin could be broken by the
capture or killing of its key men, there was danger that the
whole movement would gradually disintegrate.

As early as May 1918, a number of patriotic detectives
established a counter Intelligence system which tapped British
secret information and had it promptly relayed to Collins,
although he had not yet been appointed Director of Intelligence.
They were Eamonn Broy, who was employed in the G Division
headquarters in Brunswick Street, and Joseph Kavanagh and
James MacNamara, both of whom worked in Dublin Castle.
David Neligan, who also worked in the Castle, came in June
1920 and was later sworn into the British secret service. He
had resigned from the G Division but, persuaded by Collins
to rejoin and serve the cause of Irish independence, he passed
on some of the most vital secrets of the British forces in Ireland
to IRA Intelligence. So successful was he in the role of double
agent that the unsuspecting British awarded him a life pension.

In July 1919 the Squad was formed from a small band of
Volunteers selected by Michael Collins from different company

units of the Dublin Brigade for difficult and dangerous work in the city. It was organized and established on a firm footing by Mick McDonnell, its first Commanding Officer, who was then sent elsewhere on other important assignments. Initially, the Squad comprised five members: Mick McDonnell, Paddy O'Daly, Joe Leonard, Ben Byrne and Sean Doyle. It was soon reinforced by Jim Slattery, Vinnie Byrne, Mick O'Reilly and Tom Kehoe, a stepbrother of McDonnell. Later members included Frank Bolster, Eddie Byrne, Jimmy Conroy, Paddy Griffin, Bill Stapleton, Ned Breslin, Mick Hennessey, Johnny Dunne, Sean Coffey, Johnny Wilson and Jackie Hanlon, with Pat McCrea as part-time driver. Throughout the entire period of its operations, the Squad was commanded by Paddy O'Daly, with Joe Leonard his second in command. The Squad was whole-time and available on short notice at any hour, day or night. The members took their orders from GHQ Intelligence, which Collins himself directed and controlled. They were paid a weekly subsistence allowance of £4.10s (£4.50) out of Dáil funds. Their base was in Upper Abbey Street, a few hundred yards from Dublin Castle, and sleeping quarters were available to them in various private houses in the city. They were given no special training beyond what they had got in their own Volunteer (IRA) Units. The chief function of the Squad, but by no means the only important one, was the extermination of enemy police and military Intelligence, and native spies and touts.

Prior to the formation of the Squad, in April 1919, Collins had given the G-men peremptory notice that those who continued at political work after a certain date would be shot on sight, and on the expiry of his ultimatum and by authority of the Minister for Defence, Cathal Brugha, he ordered the Squad to execute those who had ignored the notice. Six G-men were shot dead over a period in which a number of others were wounded. They paid the penalty for their contempt of several personal warnings. The sixth was Assistant Commissioner William C. Forbes Redmond, who had been brought down specially from Belfast to reorganize the force and smash IRA Intelligence. He was shot dead near the Standard Hotel in Harcourt Street on 21 January 1920, having lasted less than a month in Dublin; his shooting brought about the initial collapse of the G Division of the DMP.

The executions were carried out in city streets in broad daylight. Two Squad members would carry out the task in co-operation with an Intelligence officer, whose part was to indicate the G-men concerned clearly and distinctly, by pre-arranged signal. Other members of the Squad would fan out to cover the two. Among the enemy secret agents, spies and touts executed by the Squad in 1919 and 1920 was the elderly Alan Bell, ostensibly a civil servant. In fact he was engaged in the dangerous business of locating and seizing Dáil Éireann funds and the National Loan. He had performed a similar service in Land League days and was believed to be high in the British secret service. Bell was taken off a crowded tram at Merrion by armed men one morning in April 1920 and shot dead. The shooting ended the attempt to seize the funds and the Loan.

In November 1920 the Squad was called upon to take a leading part in dealing with the new menace of military secret-service agents who had been brought into the war independently of Dublin Castle. Experienced operators, under direct orders from Whitehall and having no apparent connection with the British authorities in Ireland, had made their way gradually and unobtrusively into Dublin, some with their wives, and, under assumed names, had taken up residence as civilians in city hotels and in boarding-houses on the south side of the city. Known as the 'Cairo Gang', a number of them had served in a similar capacity in Egypt and Russia. They were masters of their craft and in a short time had established a formidable organization of native spies and touts from whose bits and pieces of information they built a highly efficient espionage service. They reported direct to London in code and were almost ready for a decisive strike against the Dáil Ministry and the IRA leadership in the city when Collins, whose own Intelligence rarely failed, struck first.

The menace was smashed on 21 November 1920, the day known as 'Bloody Sunday'. Sharp at nine o'clock that morning, the time fixed for the task, groups from the four line battalions of the Dublin Brigade, led by a member of the Squad as far as numbers permitted, or by a member of GHQ Intelligence, entered the Gresham and Shelbourne Hotels, and boarding-houses at 28 Earlsfort Terrace, 28 Upper Pembroke Street, 38 Upper and 22 Lower Mount Street, 92 and 119 Lower Baggot Street and 117 Morehampton Road, and accounted for eleven secret-service agents who had been condemned to die. Four others were wounded. Five agents escaped. Cathal Brugha was not fully satisfied that the evidence against fifteen others was conclusive and by Cabinet decision their names were struck off the list of thirty-five agents submitted by Collins's Intelligence officers. Also dead was an officer of the Royal Veterinary Corps, who was shot by mistake in the Gresham Hotel, and two Auxiliaries who ran into a force of IRA in Lower Mount Street.

The British took their revenge immediately. Lorry loads of Auxiliaries drove to Croke Park that afternoon and opened fire on a large crowd that was watching a football match between Dublin and Tipperary, killing fourteen and wounding more than sixty, eleven very seriously. One of the dead was Michael Hogan, the Tipperary goalkeeper.

On Saturday night, 20 November, the eve of Bloody Sunday, Commandant Dick McKee and Vice-Commandant Peadar Clancy of the Dublin Brigade were betrayed to the Dublin Castle Auxiliaries and captured in Fitzpatrick's house in Lower Gloucester Street in the early hours of Sunday morning. They had made all the arrangements for what would happen at nine o'clock that morning and now knew what would happen to themselves. Before the raiders burst in upon them, McKee had time to burn all his papers, including a list of the Intelligence officers who were condemned to die within a matter of hours. It is beyond doubt that the raiders were aware of the importance of McKee and Clancy, both of whom were also attached to GHQ, McKee as Director of Training, and Clancy as Director of Munitions. They bundled them into a lorry, with their friend Fitzpatrick, and took all three to the Castle. That afternoon a notorious pair of interrogators and torturers, Captain Hardy and Major King of the Auxiliaries F Company, picked out McKee and Clancy from a line-up of twenty-six prisoners in the Auxiliaries' guardroom. On Monday morning, McKee and Clancy, along with Conor Clune, a young Irish language enthusiast from Quin, County Clare, were taken out and shot in the narrow courtyard that led from the Auxiliaries' quarters to the military guardroom in the Castle. 'Shot while attempting to escape' was the official report issued by the British Government.

The bodies were taken to the mortuary chapel in the Pro-Cathedral. A doctor brought in that night by Collins and members of the Squad to examine them found bayonet thrusts, one of which had broken several of McKee's ribs and penetrated his liver. There were multiple bruises as well as the bullet wounds. After the medical examination, the bodies of McKee and Clancy were dressed in the uniform of the Irish Volunteers. (The remains of Clune had been removed earlier to his native County Clare.) Next morning Collins, with Tom Cullen and Frank Thornton of IRA Intelligence, and Gearoid O'Sullivan, the Adjutant-General, carried out the coffins to the waiting hearses, despite the watching enemy agents and touts. A photographer snapped a quick photograph which was published in the *Evening Herald*. It showed Collins and Cullen at the head of McKee's coffin. The Squad and others bought up all the copies of the early edition for burning and had smashed the matrix and metal plates in the *Herald* printing works before British Intelligence officers called there.

An ex-military police-sergeant named James Ryan, who lived off Gloucester Street, had for some time been suspected of spying by men of the 2nd Battalion, following the arrest of IRA members whose homes were nearby. Jimmy Brennan, C Company Quartermaster (the author's company) had sought permission to have him shot, but Tom Ennis, the Battalion OC, had refused on the grounds that there was not sufficient evidence against him at the time. Collins's Intelligence officers eventually identified him as the spy who, on the night of 20 November, had informed the Castle that McKee and Clancy had entered Fitzpatrick's. 'Shankers' Ryan, as he was known, was executed by the Squad in Hynes's pub in Gloucester Place on the morning of 5 February 1921. He was a brother of Becky

Cooper, famed in that neighbourhood as a brothel keeper.

The military secret-service organization never recovered from the blow struck on Bloody Sunday. Dublin District GHQ admitted that their 'Special Branch' had been 'temporarily paralyzed' by the attack on the agents. In the next few days, secret-service agents, their cover blown, together with minor spies, spotters and touts fleeing their haunts in terror, sought refuge in the Castle and the five or six adjoining buildings which had been taken over for the purpose of securing it against attack, and to accommodate a swarm of English civil servants and their families.

The military secret-service agents, living among the people in the guise of civilians during the war, were liable to the death penalty, apart from which fact IRA Intelligence had accumulated unmistakable evidence of their direct or indirect involvement in the murder of Irish citizens. The Cabinet had no alternative but to sanction the executions if the fight for freedom were to be won.

While the Squad, reinforced by elements of the battalions as occasion arose, continued to carry out its duties, the decision was taken to organize an active service unit within the Dublin Brigade. The ASU was formed towards the end of November 1920, and began operations early in January 1921. It consisted of fifty men selected from the four line battalions, under the command of Paddy Flanagan, with Mick White second in command, and was under the control of Oscar Traynor, who had succeeded Dick McKee as Brigade OC. The unit was organized in four sections. Each section identified with the battalion from which it was drawn and it operated in that battalion area and adjoining county districts. The individual sections as such carried out scores of attacks on military, Auxiliaries, and Black and Tans, and the entire unit was mobilized for large-scale operations which necessitated the use of a stronger force. Like the members of the Squad, the ASU men were withdrawn from their civilian jobs and employed as whole-time soldiers paid out of Dáil funds. Their coming into action as the ASU stepped up tremendously the tempo of the war in Dublin.

Following the liquidation of so many of their most important military and police spies, British Intelligence decided to form a unit of their own along the lines of the Squad. For this purpose they transferred from Galway to Dublin an able and courageous RIC officer named Eugene Igoe to take charge of a body of tough, daring policemen (RIC) who were likely to recognize important country members of the IRA whom they would arrest or shoot on the spot. The arrival of these men on the streets of Dublin greatly increased the work of the Squad and made it more perilous. They moved around the city in a body, discreetly armed and dressed in civilian clothes, usually too strong to be engaged in crowded streets, so the ASU and the battalions struck back by increasing the intensity of their attacks on enemy lorries. In the words of Paddy O'Daly, 'with the ASU carrying out ambushes and the Squad picking off spies, Dublin was a hot spot'.

Bill Stapleton, a member of the Squad, wrote this description of an action against Igoe's men for the 1969 issue of *The Capuchin Annual* (the Squad had been watching Igoe and his men for some time):

Three of Igoe's picked men were known to leave Dublin Castle for luncheon about 12.30 pm daily. They came along Parliament Street towards the Quays. We were ordered to shoot these three and we were in Essex Street West when we received the signal from the Intelligence officer. The three men, looking I thought rather weary, were walking along the footpath towards Capel Street and when they reached the top of Essex Street we fired on them and they fell. A crowd of people appeared from a side street leading to Saint Michael and Saint John's Church and were approaching Parliament Street. We pocketed our guns and ran towards them as firing started from the sentry who was on duty at the City Hall, shouting as we ran, 'Oh, don't go up there. People are shooting one another.' They paused and turned back and we mingled with them and ran on to the quayside, over the Father Mathew Bridge; we were back in George Moreland's (our base) in a matter of minutes, handling our pieces of timber as though we had never left the place. (Cabinet making was the cover). This presence of mind was something we all seemed able to produce at the right moment.

Among the many actions in which the Squad participated were the several attempts to shoot the Lord Lieutenant, Viscount French, and most daring of all, the attempted rescue of Sean MacEoin from Mountjoy jail on 14 May 1921. MacEoin was awaiting courtmartial. The death sentence was inevitable. Collins planned every detail of the rescue operation and used the Squad for the action, together with Emmet Dalton of GHQ and his brother Charlie of the Intelligence service, Peter Gough, a machine-gunner, Tom Walsh of B Company 2nd Battalion, and Aine Malone of Cumann na mBan. The plan was to capture and man an armoured car with Squad members dressed as a British crew, use the car to gain entrance to the jail, secure possession of MacEoin and ensure that the raiders got safely out of the jail. Paddy O'Daly organized the groups who would participate in the action and was in charge of the main party.

British military lorries which drew meat rations for city barracks from the Dublin abattoir several times every morning were escorted by an armoured car. The supervisor of the abattoir was Michael Lynch, OC Fingal Brigade. He reported to Collins that there were mornings when the entire crew left the car after it was parked in the abattoir yard. The driver would lock it and join the others for a smoke and a walk about. This led to the opinion that the car could be captured. Collins ordered Charlie Dalton to take up quarters in Lynch's house, which adjoined and overlooked the main yard of the abattoir. Dalton was to watch the movements of the crew from the window of an upstairs room, with the blind pulled down. If it went up it was the signal that the crew had got out of the car.

Word of what was about to happen was sent in to MacEoin through warder Breslin and he was instructed that, commencing 12 May, he should be with Governor Monroe in his office every morning from ten to eleven o'clock, on one pretext or another. That was the hour when Monroe interviewed prisoners. Collins, Emmet Dalton and Joe Leonard had a meeting with Breslin from whom they obtained precise information about the warders, the positions of the military and Auxiliary guards, their mealtimes and relief times.

On successive mornings from 12 May, Squad men and other Volunteers dressed in dungarees gave a convincing impression of Dublin Corporation employees waiting to start work at the nearby cattle market. On the third morning, Paddy O'Daly, from a position at the North Circular Road corner of Aughrim Street, saw the window blind go up. Waving his arms he raced down the street to meet the others. Suddenly the job was on. The IRA closed in, held up and disarmed the crew, shooting some who resisted. They secured the keys of the car, a big heavily armed Peerless model, which was immediately manned by Pat McCrea, driver, with Bill Stapleton his assistant, Sean Coffey and Peter Gough, machine-gunners, and Tom Kehoe, who was included for his coolness, courage and initiative in any dangerous situation. McCrea drove the car down the North Circular Road to Hanlon's Corner, where he slowed up to collect Emmet Dalton and Joe Leonard, both dressed and armed as British officers. Dalton, who had been a British officer, was carrying a forged Prisoner's Removal Order for the transfer of MacEoin to Dublin Castle. Jimmy Conroy and other Squad men held the British crew and the rations fatigue party in the abattoir. McCrea drove to Mountjoy. Dalton, who was sitting outside the car where an officer usually sat, waved his forged document at the gate-keeper. The main gate was opened wide and shut to after the car was driven inside. Two iron gates in the arched entrance to the jail were then opened. McCrea drove the car through these gates, which were about eighteen feet apart, and in one wide sweep brought it back between them, 'carelessly' jamming both open. This meant that the main gate alone barred the way out, which was exactly what Collins had planned.

A sentry stood at attention as the two 'British officers' strode into the main hall of the jail. They climbed a stairs and entered Governor Monroe's office without difficulty. It was there that the plan broke down. MacEoin, who had succeeded in being in the governor's office from ten o'clock to eleven-thirty on the previous two mornings was prevented from being there on the morning of the 14th, due to a sudden last-minute change of prison routine by the officer in charge of a new body of

Auxiliary guards. Nevertheless, all went well until Monroe decided that he must telephone Dublin Castle for confirmation of the order to remove MacEoin. As he moved to do so, Leonard sprang for the telephone and smashed it against the wall, while Dalton, drawing his gun, held Monroe and his staff at bay. At this juncture a fusillade of shots was heard. It was time to go. Dalton and Leonard left the building with all haste.

Mingling with a large crowd of people, who had gathered outside the main gate with parcels of food for their relatives and friends inside, were Frank Bolster, Tom Walsh and Aine Malone carrying a mock parcel. When the wicket gate was opened to take in her parcel at the crucial moment, Bolster and Walsh rushed the gate-keeper and opened the main gate with his keys. A sentry on the roof saw the gate being rushed and he fired a shot that wounded Walsh and raised a general alarm. Before he could fire another round the ever-alert Tom Kehoe shot him dead from the courtyard with a Peter the Painter and his rifle fell down to the pavement. Dalton and Leonard emerged running from the building, then turned about and blazed several shots along a corridor. Leonard and Kehoe jumped into the car as the Auxiliary guards were seen advancing. Stapleton followed them in with the sentry's rifle and fixed bayonet. Dalton got on to the back of the car and continued firing as McCrea drove it out of the main gate, down the drive and on to the North Circular Road.

The entire IRA party was glum and disappointed by the failure to rescue MacEoin. The 'British officers', Dalton and Leonard, still in uniform, got out of the car at North Richmond Street schools where Joe Hyland, Collins's driver, was waiting to take MacEoin away in his taxi. They got into the taxi and Hyland drove off with them. McCrea's instructions were to drive the armoured car to a point between Malahide and Swords, where it would be hidden in a big barn on the farm of a friend. The Peerless overheated badly on the way and finally spluttered to a halt midway between the upper and lower gates of what is now Clontarf Golf Club. The machine-guns were stripped from their mountings and, with the dead sentry's rifle, taken to a brigade arms dump later in the day. The crew set fire to the engine of the car and then slipped away. There was no pursuit.

The rescue attempt failed because the armoured car could only be seized when the soldiers, contrary to regulations, had left it. Had it been captured on either 12 or 13 May, MacEoin would have been in the governor's office at the appointed time. It came as a severe jolt to public opinion in England to find that the IRA could capture an armoured car from the British military, drive it straight into Mountjoy jail and escape unscathed with it in broad daylight. The rescue parties showed great daring, resourcefulness and a fierce determination not to be stopped by danger of any kind. The action made a substantial contribution to bringing about the Truce.

The Squad and the ASU mustered their full strength on 25 May 1921 to join with the 2nd Battalion of the Dublin Brigade in the most important single engagement of the whole war in the Brigade area — the burning of the Custom House. The action, for which de Valera pressed, was entirely successful, but the cost in casualties was near catastrophic — seven killed, twelve wounded and about seventy captured out of a total force of some 120. Tom Kehoe and Jimmy Conroy of the Squad were among those captured and Jim Slattery was severely wounded, as was Tom Ennis, the battalion commandant. As a result of the heavy losses, the Squad and the ASU were amalgamated to form one unit which from then on was known as 'the Guard' and was commanded by Paddy O'Daly.

INDEX

ANVIL BOOKS

TOM BARRY

Guerilla Days in Ireland

The story of the famous West Cork Flying Column told by the man who led it, Commandant -General Tom Barry. His small band of poorly armed fighters outfought and outwitted the heavily equipped army of a mighty empire. Essential reading for inside knowledge of the War of Independence.

256 pages   16pp illustrations
ISBN 0 947962 34 4

DAN BREEN

My Fight for Irish Freedom

One of the most important 'source' books for information about the Irish War of Independence, this is the personal account of one of its most famous figures, Dan Breen. The ambush at Soloheadbeg, masterminded by Dan Breen and Sean Treacy, was the spark that ignited the war in 1919.

192 pages   16pp illustrations
ISBN 0 947962 33 6

RICHARD DAVIS

Arthur Griffith and Non-Violent Sinn Féin

A scholarly and well researched study of Arthur Griffith, one of the founders of modern Ireland and founding father of Sinn Féin. With a postscript study of the principal Irish guerilla leaders 1920–21.
Richard Davis lectures in history at the University of Tasmania in Hobart.

254 pages   24 pp illustrations
ISBN 0 947962 30 1

ANVIL BOOKS

TERENCE de VERE WHITE
Kevin O'Higgins

Kevin O'Higgins, recognized as the 'strong man' of the first
Irish Government, was shot dead in July 1927.
Terence de Vere White's masterly biography fully records his
life and death, and gives a comprehensive account of the Black
and Tan period and the Treaty debates. First published in
1948, the Anvil edition of 1986 brings the book up to date.

272 pages   ISBN 0 947962 11 5

FLORENCE O'DONOGHUE
No Other Law

'We have declared for an Irish Republic and will not live under
any other law' — Liam Lynch's declaration of principle led to
the Civil War in 1922. A year later he was dead,
not yet thirty years of age.
First published in 1954, *No Other Law* is a full and factual
account of the life and times of Liam Lynch, written by a man
with inside knowledge of the period. But it is also a story as
human and personal as a novel.

368 pages   ISBN 0 947962 12 3

ERNIE O'MALLEY
On Another Man's Wound

Ernie O'Malley's memoirs of the fighting in Ireland from 1916
to 1921 was first published in 1936 in London, Boston and
Berlin. It immediately became the classic account of those
years on both sides of the Atlantic.
'The outstanding literary achievement of the Anglo-Irish war.'
Richard M. Kain.
Republished by Anvil in 1979.

336 pages   ISBN 0 947962 31 X

ANVIL BOOKS

ERNIE O'MALLEY

Raids and Rallies

An account of various offensives against the British in 1920–21
in the south and west of Ireland — Hollyford, Drangan,
Rearcross, Rineen, Scramogue, Tourmakeady, Modreeny and
Carrowkennedy.
'Where O'Malley differs from virtually all others who have
published their recollections of those years is that he was a
writer and an intellectual who was constantly weighing and
analysing all that was happening.' IRISH POST

208 pages   8pp maps
ISBN 0 900068 63 9

ERNIE O'MALLEY

The Singing Flame

This continuation of *On Another Man's Wound*, covering the
years 1922–1924, was published posthumously by Anvil in
1978. O'Malley worked on it, drafting and redrafting in the
light of new information, until his death in 1957. All his various
manuscripts and typescripts were brought together and edited
onto a comprehensive and definitive text by Frances-Mary
Blake who made a deep study of the O'Malley papers in
University College, Dublin, which she researched and sorted.

320 pages   ISBN 0 947962 33 8